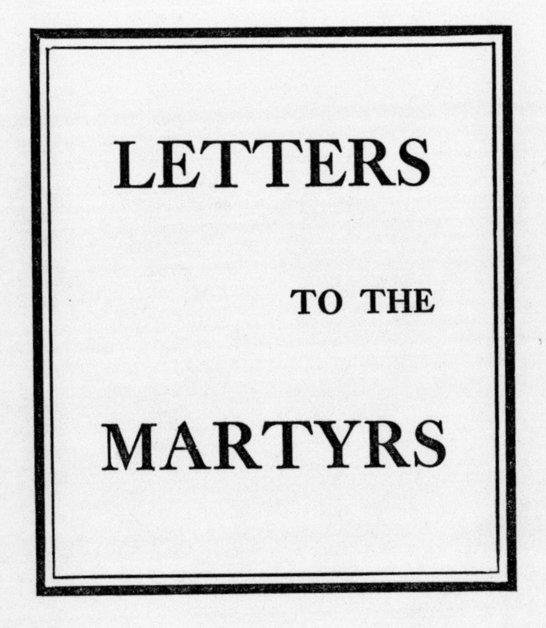
LETTERS
TO THE
MARTYRS

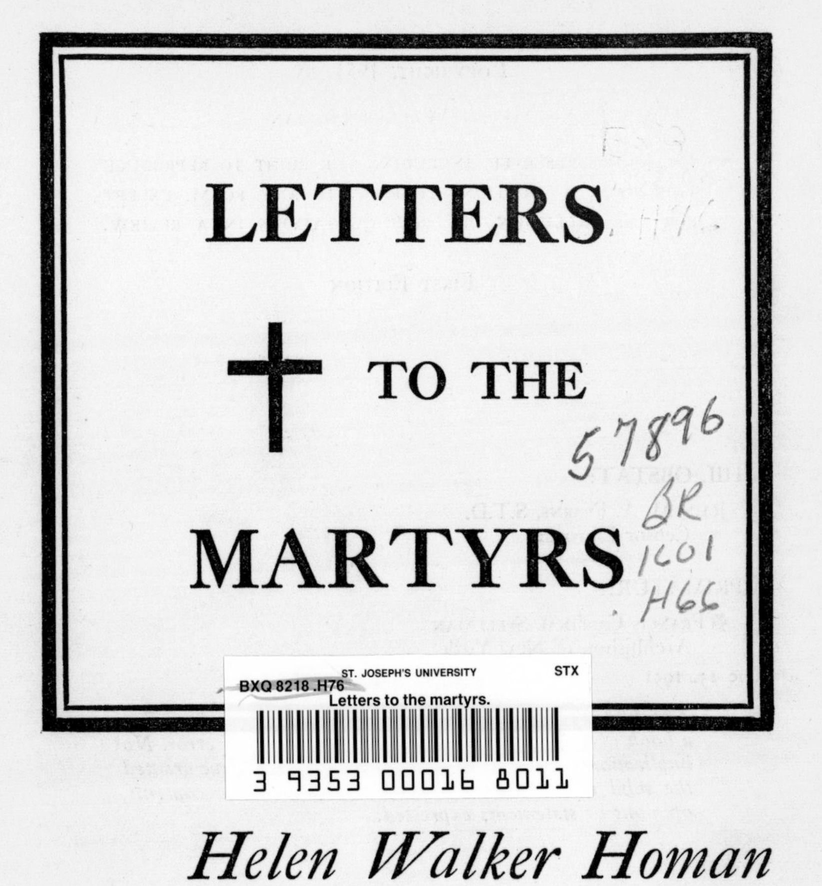

LETTERS TO THE MARTYRS

Helen Walker Homan

DAVID McKAY COMPANY, *Inc.*
NEW YORK

First Edition

NIHIL OBSTAT:

John M. A. Fearns, S.T.D.
Censor Librorum

IMPRIMATUR:

✠ Francis Cardinal Spellman
Archbishop of New York

June 15, 1951

The nihil obstat and imprimatur are official declarations that a book or pamphlet is free of doctrinal or moral error. No implication is contained therein that those who have granted the nihil obstat and imprimatur agree with the contents, opinions or statements expressed.

MANUFACTURED IN THE UNITED STATES OF AMERICA

To the Brothers

JAMES BLAINE WALKER, JR.

ROBERT WILLARD WALKER

All statements made in this book concerning the holiness of any characters mentioned are humbly submitted to the judgment of the Church, especially to the decrees of Urban VIII and other Popes.

CONTENTS

FOREWORD

Cut into the dank stone of a subterranean prison in Rome, an ancient Latin inscription reads: "Here, Peter was imprisoned as an Enemy of the State." But historians agree that Peter was actually imprisoned, as were thousands of that time, for preaching the doctrine of Jesus Christ. Peter went forth from that imprisonment to die, a martyr nailed to a cross, allegedly because he was an enemy of the State—but actually because he steadfastly proclaimed the divinity of Christ and the truth of His doctrine.

That was in the first century, Anno Domini.

Today, in the twentieth century, men again are imprisoned, are tortured and die, also allegedly for being "enemies of the State"; but again, actually because they preach the identical doctrine preached by Peter in that first Age of Martyrdom—the doctrine laid down by Jesus Christ.

Almost two thousand years later, in this, the Second Age of Martyrdom, cause, effect, and disguise are the same.

While in the twenty centuries since Peter died, a "witness" to the truth, the world has greatly changed, it is, in fundamental things, strikingly the same. As the French paradox has it, "*plus ça change, plus c'est la même chose*"—the more it changes, the more it's the same.

Since Stephen, the first "witness"—he of the face of an angel—died, a crumpled and bleeding mass from the stones which killed him, and proclaiming with his last breath the Risen

Christ, the Christian world has cherished the memory of its martyrs. Today, it has found new martyrs to cherish—its own contemporaries.

Stephen's fidelity and heroism are dramatically matched in our time by the fidelity and heroism of such men as Cardinal Mindszenty of Hungary, and Archbishop Stepinac of Yugoslavia who have suffered something perhaps worse than death. The actual martyrdoms of such men as Father Miguel Pro, a Jesuit of Mexico; Maximilian Kolbe, a Franciscan of Poland; Alfred Delp, a Jesuit of Germany; Gerard Donovan, Maryknoll missioner of the United States; and Bishop Florentino Barroso of Spain, along with thousands of others in terror-dominated lands who have died for upholding the principles of Christ, are strikingly like those of the first Christian martyrs.

Today, as then, an "enemy of the State" in lands where the State has attempted to supplant God, has come to mean a defender of Christ. Fundamentals do not change. And today Christian virtues are held by many to be as obnoxious as they were held in the first ages of persecution. In the fourth century, Saint Agnes, the child-martyr, died to preserve her virginity. In the twentieth century, Maria Goretti died for the same reason.

Saint Ignatius of Antioch who was devoured by lions because he upheld the authority of Christian Bishops; Saint Lawrence the jester who was burned alive because he loved the poor; the fortieth Martyr of Sebaste who for love of Christ flung himself voluntarily into a frozen death; Saint Lucian who consecrated the Bread and Wine with bound hands as he faced martyrdom; Saint Thomas the Apostle, who was killed on a high mountain in the East because he was a missioner of Christ; and Saint Sebastian whose body was made a living target for archers because he preached the Risen Christ in defiance of imperial edict—all have their modern prototypes.

As for the moderns who by their courage have actually courted martyrdom as did the early Christians, our Holy Father, Pope Pius XII, stands in the foremost rank. When as Archbishop Pacelli in 1919 he was Papal Nuncio in Munich and the Communists invaded his residence, threatening to kill him, he was the first to greet them, knowing that at any moment he might be shot down. Something in his calm, fearless attitude defeated them. Later, as Pope during the second World War, he courted martyrdom constantly when the bombs rained upon Rome, and he turned a deaf ear to all proposals to seek safety elsewhere. Thirty-three of his predecessors in Saint Peter's Chair were martyrs. It would seem as though he desired to be the thirty-fourth.

In a sense, this Second Age of Martyrs is even greater than the First. For the persecution today is more intense and far-flung; its inclusion of countries and peoples, more vast; its victims numerically far greater.

In 200 years of persecution, from Nero to Diocletian, 2,000,000 martyrs died. In 30 years of persecution, under Communism and allied atheism, more than 20,000,000 have died.

The martyrs of the First Age of Martyrdom became the heroes of Christian literature. Ours of the Second Age of Martyrdom, whose glory so nearly parallels theirs, will also become, in the long perspective of history, heroes of Christian literature. And many will undoubtedly come to be venerated as saints. For in spite of the new yet ever ancient war against Christ, the Cross will triumph. Neither the gates of hell nor the Iron Curtain shall prevail against it. The dark era shall pass. And the blood of the new martyrs, as that of the old, shall glorify His Kingdom.

For these are the brothers and sisters of Peter and Paul—of Stephen and Sebastian—of Agnes and Cecilia—alike not alone in sanctity, but so alike in human characteristics as to be truly brothers in flesh and blood; flesh tortured, and blood spilled lavishly for the love of Jesus Christ.

HELEN WALKER HOMAN

New York
Feast of Saint Catherine of Siena
April 30, 1951

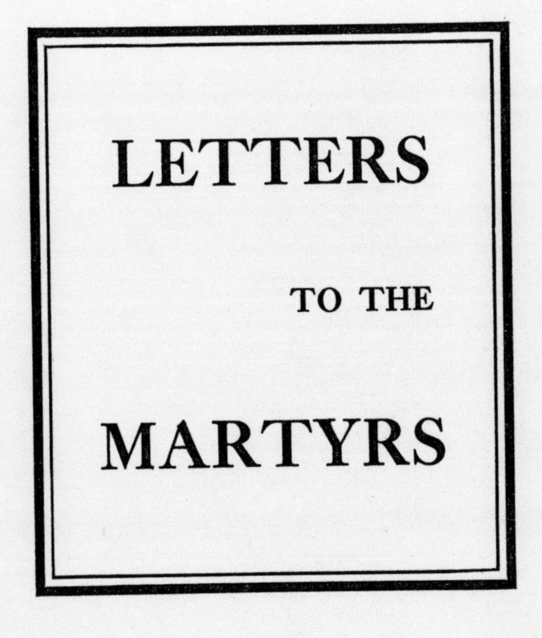
LETTERS
TO THE
MARTYRS

I

To the First Martyr,
Saint Stephen
concerning **ARCHBISHOP STEPINAC OF YUGOSLAVIA**

Dear Saint Stephen:

When I was young, I wrote some letters to some saints. As far as I know, there have been no reprisals; though as the years have passed and brought with them, it may be hoped, some measure of discretion, I have frequently wondered why.

Yet when such thoughts approach, immediately there comes the realization that the saints are, as we employ the term here below, very human: completely understanding of all frailties, many having themselves once battled and conquered these. They above all who ever lived upon earth, understand the Master's compassion and even tenderness for the simplicity of human nature with its weakness and absurdities.

Being an American, and young, at that time I thought we could go right up and speak to anyone to whom we had taken a fancy, and that they would be glad to meet us. "All men are created free and equal." That was before I had learned that the Creator's plan was one thing, but that man had twisted it into an ugly shape called enslavement. I was so certain my letters would receive instant attention.

But later I was to encounter those political movements which have bedeviled my country during the past twenty years, and soon became the victim of such urgent behests as: "Write a letter to your Congressman!" I've learned a lot,

Saint Stephen, since I wrote those first letters to the saints. But I am more convinced than ever, that even if Congressmen don't bother to read letters, saints surely do.

And so to you, dear Saint Stephen, and with utter confidence, do I address this letter—because you have been in my thoughts constantly for the past ten years or more; in fact, since the Second Age of Martyrdom came upon this earth. For, to your everlasting glory, it was you who inaugurated the First Age of Martyrdom—and between the two, despite all the centuries which have intervened, there is a startling similarity. I'm sure it must have struck you, Saint Stephen.

Much time passed before I realized that the very word "martyr" means "witness." As Paul Allard has put it, "a witness even to certainty; that is, if the greatest sign of certainty be to sacrifice our lives to prove the truth of what we affirm."

And that is precisely what you did, Saint Stephen, on that long-ago day when they dragged you, a youthful disciple, from your trial before the Sanhedrin, outside the city gates of Jerusalem where they killed you with stones—even as they would kill a snake.

M. Allard declares that the word "martyr," in the sense in which we accept it today, was unknown before the Christian Gospel came into the world. In the first years of the Church, it signified the occular witnesses of the death and Resurrection of Christ who testified to these publicly; and later came to signify those who accepted these facts on the testimony of others, and in turn gave testimony to their belief. Christ had said: "You will be hated by all men for My Name's sake, but he that shall endure until the end, shall be saved." When not long after, His faithful friends, standing staunch in their testimony, were tortured and put to death, the word took on the additional significance of one who gladly accepts death as the ultimate testimony he can give to affirm the truth he believes.

Now from the time I was very young, martyrs absorbed me. Gradually I learned they did not all belong to ancient times. As the years unfolded, first there was Mexico, where holy men and women died gloriously, under the decrees of a neo-Communism, for their faith. Then there was Spain, where they did likewise under a more positive Communism stemming directly from Moscow; latterly there was Germany where they died for both race and religion under the god of State; and now there is Russia and all Soviet-dominated areas of Europe and Asia where they have died by the millions because they believe in God. . . .

Is it any wonder that I began to think more and more about you, Saint Stephen? For it was you who almost two thousand years ago, set the pattern of Christian martyrdom. And now I am wondering, as you look down upon this sick old earth, just what you are thinking of our modern martyrs. Are you not paralleling their case to yours—measuring their standards of heroism by those set by you and His first followers? Are they measuring up, Saint Stephen? Somehow I seem to hear your warm assent. It is as though I were to ask a veteran of the first World War, what he thinks of the boys who fought our second World War. Myself, I was rather partial to the boys of the first war—it was my generation, you see—but whenever I have asked this question of the first war's veterans, they have almost bitten my head off. "We did nothing!" they say. "These boys of World War II really took the punishment, and gave it!" That is the way with heroes. They always tell you that someone else did the task better than they.

And so it is, Saint Stephen, that I rather think you admire the Christian martyrs of the twentieth century, and also believe you have stood by the side of many, giving them courage in their "testimony."

I'm sure all of them have thought of you when their hour of trial has come. The remarkable thing is, that the pattern of persecution has changed so slightly! Two thousand years are as but a day; and so much of what happened to you then, has been repeated within our own time.

How your story comes to life today! It's a wonderful story; and as I was reading it again the other night, somehow it suggested the figure of Archbishop Stepinac who is giving *his* testimony at this very hour. I seem to see a similarity between what has befallen him in the twentieth century, and what befell the great protomartyr of the first century. I wonder, Saint Stephen, if you would agree that there is even a close personal parallel between you—that you share many characteristics in common? Even your names are alike—Stephen and Stepinac. Is it possible that his draws its origin from yours?

They have not yet taken his life—he is in some strange, far prison, we are told, in Yugoslavia—condemned to sixteen years of imprisonment. About five of those years have already passed, and now he is fifty-three years old. He will be sixty-four, when he completes his sentence, if he lives that long. But it will be a further five years before he can regain his civic and political rights. Then, he will be sixty-nine. His property, he will never regain. That was confiscated when the sentence was imposed.

And though up to the present he cannot be termed a martyr in the glorious sense that you are, so many of his experiences parallel your own, that I feel sure he must have pondered much upon your life, and from it drawn inspiration.

He would have thought first about your youth, Saint Stephen, and of how you came to follow Jesus of Nazareth.

That you were a Jew who had been brought up in some land where Greek was the native tongue seems to be accepted by all. You are called a "Hellenist of the Dispersion," which somehow seems to carry a great dignity with it; and, we are told that the very name "Stephen" is Greek.

While we know that as a young man, you had found your way to Jerusalem, it is only legend which tells us that you had gone there to study "the law and the prophets" under that wise and gentle old rabbi, "a pharisee named Gamaliel, a doctor of the law, respected by all the people." Some scholars have accepted this view because your masterly defense at the trial, as reported in the Acts, showed the logic of a well-trained mind—and since Gamaliel was the most famous teacher of his time, they think it probable that you were one of his pupils. For my part, I want very much to think you were.

For Gamaliel emerges from the great story of the Apostolic Age as a most appealing personality. Did he not try to temper the fanaticism of the Sanhedrin, bent on destroying the followers of Jesus, by counseling: ". . . refrain from these men, and let them alone; for if this work be of men, it will come to naught; but if it be of God, you cannot overthrow it, lest perhaps you be found even to fight against God"? Stop them he did—but only for a space. . . .

When, some four hundred years after your death, the priest Lucian discovered your long-forgotten tomb, he found it near a place called "the Village of Gamaliel." He declared that Gamaliel himself appeared to him in a dream, and directed him to the tomb, where he found the name "Kelil" engraved in the stone—and knew you lay there because Kelil is the Aramaic for Stephen. And there, right next to you, lay the remains of Gamaliel. It is very pleasant to think that you two must have always been friends from the time you were a young student in Jerusalem.

But there is one other name, yet more distinguished, and even more dramatically attached to your story—first clinging to it with shame and horror, and later with glory—and that is the name of Saul of Tarsus, who became Paul. How often I have thought of the web of destiny woven by a Divine Hand which first drew you two together in violence and death, and how that death, your own, was the precurser to the rebirth of Saul whose soul had all but perished.

The words stand out starkly in the Acts:

"And casting him forth without the city, they stoned him; and the witnesses laid down their garments at the feet of a young man whose name was Saul. . . . And Saul was consenting to his death."

Although it is not written, I've always thought that Saul's great conversion began then and there; first with his reluctant admiration of your magnificent courage and of the persistence with which you cried out your "testimony" up until your last breath. And next, with the shame he must have felt, as he crept away—though still stubbornly bent upon making "havoc of the church, entering in from house to house and dragging away men and women." And when the Lord came to him there on the road to Damascus, and smote him from his horse and struck him blind, I'm certain his heart cried out for forgiveness for his part in your death.

But your story runs ahead of me. I think of you then, as one of Gamaliel's most brilliant pupils to whose eager young ears had somehow come the story of Jesus of Nazareth. Nowhere is it written that you had ever seen the Master except in visions. You were not one of His chosen Twelve who had walked and worked with Him before the dark shadow of Calvary fell upon them all. But you were one upon whom, shortly thereafter, the luminous light of the Resurrection had fallen; and you had cast all else aside to become a disciple. I often wonder which one of the Twelve it was who converted you. I rather like to think it was Peter—Peter who was so lovable, and so great. Possibly you were one of the three thousand whom Peter converted in a day, following the visitation of the Holy Spirit and the gift of tongues, when those Twelve unlettered men suddenly began to speak in all languages.

However it was, you cast your lot with them, these friends of the Master, and helped them to establish the infant Church. What a change from your former life! For now you lived with the group in Jerusalem, "persevering in the doctrine of the Apostles, and in the communication of the breaking of the bread, and in prayers." And you witnessed the signs and wonders wrought by the Apostles in His Name—Jesus of Nazareth, the Son of the Living God.

There in that early group, as has often been said, was the first "communism"; but how different from the Communism of today! "And all they that believed were together, and had all things in common. Their possessions and goods they sold, and divided them all, according as every one had need. And continuing daily with one accord in the Temple, and breaking bread from house to house, they took their meat with gladness and simplicity of heart; praising God, and having favor with all the people."

Yet, as you found favor with the people, you lost it with the leaders of the synagogues and the high priests. The more miracles which were wrought by the Apostles, the more crippled who leapt up and walked, the more dour did the orthodox leaders become. All the people were flocking to the doctrine of Him of whom the leaders spoke derisively as "the Nazarene."

Of course, as in any communal group, it was necessary among the first Christians that certain should be charged with special responsibilities—some intellectual, some menial. I find it charming, Saint Stephen, that you, the scholar, had recognized a need and had quietly begun in a practical way to assist in the ministration of food. Not only did the Apostles and disciples have to eat, but the poor as well, and the widows. It would seem that, with the number of followers increasing every day, the matter of meals became a major problem.

Then arose that first murmuring among the group. The Greeks began to complain that their widows were being neglected at table; that the Hebrew widows were being favored. The poor Apostles, distracted at the sign of this first rift in the holy company, were forced to evolve a plan. Speaking for themselves, they said: "It is not reason that we should leave preaching the word of God, and serve tables." For great as was the hunger for food, even greater was the hunger for the Word. So they instructed the group to select "seven men of good reputation, full of the Holy Ghost and wisdom, whom we may appoint over this business."

It was indeed, what might be called a "business," Saint Stephen! It would seem that by this time you had won the trust and affection of the entire group, Hebrew and Greek alike, and that you must have been elected unanimously. For in the Acts, yours is the first name mentioned. "And they chose Stephen, a man full of faith, and of the Holy Ghost." So it was that I came early to think of you as both scholarly and humble; as unselfish, trustworthy, and practical. But courage was your crowning characteristic. It enkindled a flame that has not died in almost two thousand years. And it is no wonder your companions loved you.

I have often speculated about those other "men of good reputation" who were chosen with you. Of course, we know that Philip was a great disciple, and it is said too, that you and he were close friends. Some day I hope you will tell me about Prochorus and Nicanor, Timon and Pharmenas, and "Nicolas, a proselyte of Antioch."

Of you seven, it is related: "These they set before the Apostles; and they praying, imposed hands upon them." Thus chosen by the group, was this perhaps the first time in Christian history when occurred that symbolic bestowal of authority, the "laying on of hands"?

With your appointment as deacon (as some would call you), supervising the distribution of food, the Greek widows could no longer complain at table and disturb everyone's digestion. Or if they did, you could easily placate them, because your native tongue was the same as theirs.

Converts began to come in scores, and what was even better for the strategic position of the group, "a great multitude also of the priests obeyed the faith." Alas, if they could only have been more!

It was at that time that you came into your great power. "And Stephen, full of grace and fortitude, did great wonders and signs among the people." That meant, of course, miracles. You had come to share with the Apostles that glorious prediction of the Master:

"And these signs shall follow them.... In My Name they shall cast out devils: they shall speak with new tongues. They shall take up serpents; and if they shall drink any deadly thing, it shall not hurt them: they shall lay their hands upon the sick, and they shall recover."

But while all this caused you to be beloved by the people, it did not make you popular with the authorities. I'm sure you heard the mutterings and sensed the danger; but the odd part is, you didn't seem to care at all! The more they glowered, the harder you preached. Then it was that they began to try to refute your preaching—the synagogues of the Libertines, the Cyrenians, the Alexandrians, some of Cilicia and Asia, "disputing with Stephen." The debates were brilliantly one-sided; in fine, your opponents could offer no arguments to outweigh those which held your audiences spellbound. Victory lay in your hands; your enemies, untouched by the

Gospel of Jesus, had no conception of the mystical source of your power, the Holy Spirit, even if some recognized in your mastery of logic a mind trained by the intellectual Gamaliel.

With hurt pride, having lost face with the populace, and stung by envy, your enemies began to plot your destruction. "They suborned men to say they had heard him speak words of blasphemy against Moses and against God." Which, of course, was the farthest thing from your intent. You had merely been trying to teach them to pay less attention to the letter of the law, and more to the spirit. Alas, in our own time, in this Second Age of Martyrs, we have seen constantly how the simplest words can be twisted and transformed into a synthetic "treason"!

You were preaching the doctrine of Christ, and they did not like it, even as they don't like it today. In modern Yugoslavia, it was Archbishop Stepinac's Pastoral Letters which got them down, for in these he affirmed and reaffirmed the rights of the individual before God—the equality of all races—conversions through faith and not through fear—feeding the hungry, sheltering the refugee, protecting the homeless—God above State. This is the Gospel which the Son of God came upon earth to teach. It has not changed in two thousand years. Nor has the pattern of the persecution changed, although today its excuses are usually camouflaged, being pinned to politics rather than to religion. But the persecutors are still after the same thing: the destruction of the principles of Christ.

Only five years ago, poor Archbishop Stepinac was accused by Tito of plotting against the State, but actually his grave offense was an unflagging insistence upon the principles of Christianity. It had been the same with you; yet, *you* were accused of blasphemy against Moses and against God. Even as with Stepinac, in your case also "they stirred up the people

. . . and running together they took him, and brought him to the council." That "stirring up of the people" today is called propaganda, but its technique is the same.

I often wonder if, when they came to get you, they did not find you humbly serving the poor at table. Even though you could preach rings around them, you were following the pattern of the Great Preacher who had stopped to wash the feet of His disciples. You were not one to cavil at serving the poor their food. We have seen no accounts of Hitler or Stalin or Tito personally waiting on the poor. But we have seen accounts of their subornation of witnesses, which played its sinister part in your own story: "And they set up false witnesses, who said: 'This man ceaseth not to speak words against the holy place and the law.' For we have heard him say, that this Jesus of Nazareth shall destroy this place, and shall change the traditions which Moses delivered unto us."

Then began your great defense which was actually not a defense but a blistering accusation. Orators down the centuries have taken it as a model of argument and eloquence.

First you gave a scholarly survey of Israel's religious history, showing that its religious *forms* had from the start been relative, and subject to change; therefore there was no blasphemy in claiming that yet another change had come about with the advent of the Messias. Then you dealt, as only a scholar could, with the experiences of Moses, and showed how the Children of Israel had brought suffering upon themselves through disregard of his teaching. Had they truly kept the law, now they would be compelled to believe in Jesus whose Gospel you proclaimed.

How those important judges of the Sanhedrin must have writhed, when you cried to them: "You stiff-necked and uncircumcised in heart and ears, you always resist the Holy Ghost: as your fathers did, so do you also! Which of the prophets have not your fathers persecuted? And they have slain them who foretold of the coming of the Just One; of whom you have been now the betrayers and murderers!"

There was nothing faltering about your "testimony." Nor does the quaint language of the Acts leave anything to be imagined of the horrible scene which followed: "Now hearing these things, they were cut to the heart, and they gnashed with their teeth at him."

It was evidence of the Master's love, that you did not even see them. For instantly you looked upward, and there saw, in vision, the Messias you had loved and served so loyally. "Behold," you cried joyously, "I see the heavens opened, and the Son of Man standing on the right hand of God!"

That was the last straw. "And they, crying out with a loud voice, stopped their ears, and with one accord ran violently upon him. And casting him forth without the city, they stoned him."

We know that, according to the Jewish law, stoning was the death to be meted out to all blasphemers. But there is a doubt among scholars, whether at this point mob rule held sway, or whether they were following the due process of their own law. It does seem odd, Saint Stephen, that if they were behaving according to the law, they should have cast you forth "without the city."

To be sure, one authority states that the law required the offender to be "placed on an elevation from whence, with hands bound, he was to be thrown down"–and perhaps the most favored place lay outside the city. Yet we both know that some years later, they cast the Apostle, Saint James the Just, who also died to give the testimony of a martyr, from a pinnacle of the Temple.

Of what then, were your murderers fearful? The Roman governors were under strict orders to permit the Jews the full exercise of their religious laws, provided it did not interfere with orderly government. So it would seem that something about the proceedings had been irregular. Perhaps they feared the fury of the populace whose suffering you had relieved, and to whom you had brought cures and miracles; or of the poor, to whose hunger you had daily ministered.

But at least in one aspect, the law was observed; for it decreed that the witnesses who accused a blasphemer, should be the first to lay hands on him. That must have been why "the witnesses laid down their garments at the feet of Saul." Somewhere it is related that they thrust upon you "a stone as much as two men could carry," yet in spite of this, and while they were at their unholy work, you continued to invoke the Name which only further increased their fury. "Lord Jesus, receive my spirit!"

Thus, to the last, you gave your testimony—that testimony which is the sign of the martyr.

"And falling on his knees, he cried with a loud voice, saying: 'Lord, lay not this sin to their charge.' " You would follow the Master's example to the very end. Had He not said, as He hung upon the cross: "Father, forgive them, for they know not what they do"?

Thus gloriously did you, the First Martyr die, and go to a reward that "eye hath not seen, nor ear heard." For you were the protomartyr and had marked the great path down which so many would follow, giving testimony that Jesus Christ is the Son of God. "He that would find his life, shall lose it." Happy Saint Stephen! . . .

And Saul, who became Paul, wondered. What was that you had said, as you were dying? "Lord, lay not this sin to their charge." Why, that was strange—revolutionary! What about the law, "an eye for an eye; and a tooth for a tooth"? It was all very disturbing. . . . Then there was that extraordinary light which had illumined your face, at the trial, and upon your death. "And all . . . saw his face as if it had been the face of an angel." You were mad; that was the only explanation. Little did he then dream that he would one day do even as you had done.

All this transpired, so tradition relates, outside the Damascus Gate. And it was from the Damascus Gate that Saul would ride forth to take the road to that city, bearing a white fury against the Christians it sheltered.

Is it remarkable then, that I have thought the martyrs of our own day have pondered upon your life, Saint Stephen? Or that Archbishop Stepinac who shares many of your characteristics, must frequently turn to you for encouragement in his long imprisonment; in prayers for his country which he deeply loves? Will you not help him, Saint Stephen?

Trivial though it may be, I have even found a certain fascination in the name of the city in which he labored, and near which he was born–Zagreb. It sounds like some fabulous place out of the Arabian Nights; and I cannot but feel that the country in which he grew up as a boy, has a mysterious, ancient charm. I have imagined that when still a child, and exploring the woods as children will, he might have felt a boy's thrill of discovery upon coming suddenly into a clearing and there finding an ancient castle, with ruined turret stair, and battlements. The birds about Zagreb must bear brilliantly colored plumage; and the peasants' costumes, at least when Aloysius Stepinac was a boy, must have been colorful and picturesque.

It is said that near this capital of Croatia-Slavonia (which became Yugoslavia), vineyards and country houses abound. About them circle the high mountains. A city has been there since Roman times. The very places from which the great Archbishop consistently defied the flouters of Christ and issued his famous Pastoral Letters are romantic: the ancient Bishop's Palace, and the fifteenth-century Gothic cathedral surrounded by towers of an eleventh-century fortress. . . . When he had been but three years old, he had lived through a violent earthquake which shook the old city to its very roots. It foreshadowed in a way the events he would live to face. . . .

Born the seventh child of peasant farmers in the neighboring little village of Krashitz (he was one of eleven), young Aloysius grew up in the environs of an old and beautiful culture. It was in the month of Our Lady, on May 8, 1898, that he entered the world.

Though still little more than a child, he was a soldier in the Hungarian army in World War I; fought on the Italian front, where he was taken prisoner; and eventually ended in the Serbian army, fighting against the Germans. He emerged a second lieutenant, having won a rare and highly coveted military decoration. As with you, Saint Stephen, from the start, courage was his outstanding characteristic.

It is said that his holy peasant mother early gave herself over to prayers and to pious fasts, that one day this prized son would become a priest. At first Aloysius was attracted by the idea; but later, after he became a soldier, he thought little of it.

When the wars were over, he would take up the land, as his parents had done. However, when hostilities ceased, he completed his classical studies, and then entered the College of Economics at Zagreb, determined to study scientific agriculture. Then suddenly in 1924, that inner, soundless Voice called again—and for him there was no longer any alternative. . . . For the Master's sake, and for his country, he must prepare well, he told himself. So it was through seven long years that he became one of the most brilliant students in Rome. I'm sure that even as a student, he thought much of you, and your days of study at the feet of the gentle Gamaliel. Both of you were primarily spiritual, primarily intellectual.

He was ordained in Rome, on the Feast of Christ the King, October 26, 1930; and received the degrees of doctor of philosophy and doctor of theology. He was thirty-two years old, but with that sort of premature age which marks those who have lived at the very heart of the tragedy of war.

Like you also, his first thought when studies were completed, was of the poor. Laboring in tenements and ruins, up and down the poor streets of his beloved Zagreb, into squalor and into filth, into sickrooms and deathrooms, he brought the message of the Master. There was so much to be done! The days and nights were not long enough. He must feed the hungry poor, even as you had fed them long ago.

To start the flow of charity where it was most needed, he established that famous organization which he called "Caritas." (Could love be known by any word more beautiful?) It is extraordinary that in but four years, the fame of his work had spread even to Rome. It was Pope Pius XI who made him Titular Archbishop of Nicopsis, in 1934—and at that time he was the youngest archbishop in all the world. When you too, were very young, there had been that "laying on of hands." . . .

Scarcely three years later, in 1937, this son of peasants was named Archbishop of Zagreb.

Throughout the terrible war years that followed, when Hitler's armies occupied Yugoslavia, he consistently defied the Nazis by denouncing the persecution of the Jews—as he denounced that of all minorities. Refugees fled to him; he dispensed his own money lavishly, here helping one to go East, there, West; paying for the travel and subsistence; helping all toward rehabilitation; risking his own neck. It is related that he even helped Communists fleeing Germany. Protestant,

Catholic, or Jew, it was all one to the Archbishop; they were his brothers, and in need. There is a lovely story of a group of elderly Jews to whom he extended safety and shelter. When, at length, the international relief organizations sprang into action, and these poor people were offered egress to a safer land, they refused to go. They would rather, they said, stay near the Archbishop.

To his powers of organization, he added the powers of a diplomat, handling with marked success the kaleidoscopic military who came hot on each others' heels to Yugoslavia—through surrender, through occupation; threading his way in and out of the complex political picture. His voice rang out constantly from the grand old cathedral, in defense of Christian principles, and the Gestapo dared not silence him. He was constantly demanding of the military humane treatment of prisoners; and his words were loud and long against the extermination of Jews, their mass deportation to concentration camps.

So it was, that like you, he began to be very unpopular with the authorities. But he kept flinging his denunciations in their teeth, once even walking into the office of the head of the Quisling regime in Croatia, one Pavelitch, and addressing him with a single sentence: "It is God's command: Thou shalt not kill!" He turned about and left the startled Pavelitch as abruptly as he had come.

When the Germans decreed that all of Jewish blood should wear the yellow "Star of David," two priests and six nuns of his archdiocese who were of Jewish origin began also to wear it. But there arose such a tumult among the people at this, that the Nazis quickly exempted these religious from wearing the unpopular insignia. Quickly and sternly came the Archbishop's rebuke. From the pulpit he declared: "I have ordered these priests and nuns to continue wearing this sign of belonging to the people from whom Our Saviour was born!"

His pronouncements rang with your own fervor, the fervor of the First Martyr, the fervor of the Apostles. "To the lowering of the dignity of man, and of his worth, no human being can agree without a struggle."

When he protested the German practice of holding whole regions responsible for acts of sabotage, then the Nazis began to close in on him. Pavelitch had him imprisoned; priests who read his sermon were held under house arrest for several days; the Nazi-controlled press attacked him violently; newspapers were forbidden to report anything he said. Was it not like a recurrence of your own time, Saint Stephen, when "they stirred up the people" against you?

It is reported that there were only three occasions of Nazi violence which Stepinac did not protest: when an archiepiscopal estate was plundered; when his parents' home was destroyed; and when his own brother was arrested, accused of Communism and collaboration with the Partisans—and executed by the Germans on November 23, 1943.

But his greatest persecution was to come with the advent of the Communists and Tito. He had boldly declared: "Believe me, I know Communism. It is a satanic totalitarianism of terror, much more logical in the pursuit of its aims than Fascism ever was." His Pastoral Letter issued jointly with the Archbishop of Sarajevo and the Bishops of Banjaluka, Djakovo, and Krizhevtzi, in March of 1945, charged the Communists bluntly with having exterminated with fire and sword, "priests and the more eminent of the faithful . . . Perpetually shall the blood of these heroic martyrs cry out in accusations against those who grasp murder as a means of power." . . .

I am sure you, too, have thought of these martyrs, dear Saint Stephen. On one occasion, the Archbishop spoke of two hundred and forty-three who had been killed, and one hundred and sixty-nine who were in prison, saying: "The tribunals pronounced these death sentences after summary trial; the accused often did not know with what they were charged until the actual trial. Frequently they were denied any defense, and not permitted to call witnesses or to have legal assistance."

Again he declared: "Death sentences were inflicted for having held divergent political opinions. . . . The number of those priests put to death is greater than that of the victims of any massacre known in Balkan history for centuries."

But his gravest anxiety was for the children. "In the schools, atheism is being openly taught and religion mocked. . . . The symbol of our Redemption, the Crucifix, has been banned." Land mines were planted near a sacred native shrine; at least one child was blown to bits. "Savage outrages . . . have been committed against the dead. The bodies of some of the priests murdered by the Communists were hacked to pieces and thrown into the sea. . . . Every one of the archbishops and bishops in Yugoslavia has been arrested and held in prison."

So in the words of Archbishop Stepinac himself, has the Second Age of Martyrs come upon this earth, Saint Stephen. The result in poor Yugoslavia alone was shown in the statistics for the years 1939 and 1946. In 1939, there were more than nineteen hundred Catholic priests in the country. In 1946, scarcely four hundred. Three hundred and sixty-nine priests had been killed; one hundred and seventy-five, imprisoned; four hundred and nine, exiled; five hundred and sixty-two were missing.

Catholic nuns also suffered; but the most appalling statistics covered the Catholic laity. In Croatia alone, it was estimated that four hundred thousand had died, and more than one hundred thousand had been imprisoned during these years.

It was late in 1945 that Tito started on the Archbishop in

earnest, carefully building up his propaganda the while. First he ordered his arrest and imprisonment for seventeen days, on the charge of being an enemy of the State. When released, he was kept for months a virtual prisoner in his residence. Finally, on September 18, 1946, ten days after his particularly courageous Pastoral Letter on Christian education of youth and the basic rights of religious freedom, he was again arrested and charged with "crimes against the people." The charges sought to link him with the leaders of the independence movement in Yugoslavia.

Of course, Saint Stephen, the charges were built up on coincidences, unavoidable in the career of any man as active in public life as was the Archbishop. Slight events were magnified; casual words and chance meetings transformed into a gigantic political plot. The Archbishop had but six days to prepare his defense; the Communists had been preparing their case for nearly a year. From his arrest to his conviction on October 11, 1946, he was allowed to see his counsel only once, and then for but an hour.

The trial would strike one as ludicrous by any Western standards, were it not for its tragedy. The four judges were "packed," as was the courtroom. The Archbishop was made the subject of sneers and jests. Suborned witnesses arose, as they had in your own case, and swore falsely against the accused. Some of these were men he had befriended; indeed some of them were priests. Alas, those poor souls were also on trial; many of them had been tortured into giving false testimony. The stuff of martyrs is not meted out to the many.

But it was during the course of that trial, in the "People's Court of Croatia," that mockery of justice, that Archbishop Stepinac showed his greatest similarity to you. When finally permitted to answer his accusers, he delivered an address which lasted thirty-eight minutes, and which, like yours, was a devastating indictment of the court and the party it represented. Verbally he tore them limb from limb, assuring them the while that at any moment he was ready to die. "If we have to perish, well then we shall perish while doing our duty." . . .

With defiance he told them: "It does not trouble my conscience for issuing a certificate of free movement to Reverend Father Maritch, for I did not do so for the purpose of creating disorder. For such a 'crime' I should go to the other world with my soul at peace. Whether you believe me or not, does not matter. The accused Archbishop of Zagreb knows not only how to suffer but also how to die for his convictions. . . .

"Again I declare: Between two hundred and sixty and two hundred and seventy priests have been killed by the National Liberation Front. There exists no civilized country in the world where so many priests would have been put to death for such 'crimes' as you have brought up against them. . . . The Reverend Father Povolnjak was killed like a dog in the street, without any trial at all."

He reviled them for confiscation of Church schools, for looting the seminaries, for destroying the Catholic press, for liquidating the orphanages and homes for the poor; for limiting religious instruction, for introducing civil marriage, for seizure of lands.

"The sad thing is this," he said. "Not a single bishop, not a single priest in this country knows in the morning if he will be alive that evening; nor knows at night if he will see the light of dawn."

Of the torments inflicted upon a certain bishop, he declared: "I myself experienced the same in Zapresitch when I was attacked with stones and revolvers."

Stones. When they came raining down upon him, he must also have thought of you, Saint Stephen, and prayed.

"According to your understanding, materialism is the only

worthwhile system. And that means erasure of God and of Christianity. If there is nothing but matter—then, thank you for your 'freedom'!"

His conclusion was as though you had inspired it. "In the classrooms it is officially taught—in defiance of all historical proofs—that Jesus Christ never existed. Know you then: Jesus Christ is God! And for Him we are ready to die!" Again, the testimony of the true martyr, that same "witnessing" you uttered yourself as they beat you down with stones.

"As to myself and the verdict," he finally declared, "I seek no mercy!"

It was not his fault that they did not kill him then and there. Their fury was as great as that of your own judges of the Sanhedrin when they "gnashed with their teeth." But they dared not go as far. For while the trial was still in progress, a highly placed Communist had declared: "We cannot shoot him, as we should like to do, because he is an archbishop. But he will go to prison."

So the sentence was sixteen years of forced labor. Wherever he is, dear Saint Stephen, I hope you will comfort him; for Archbishop Stepinac of Zagreb is one of the greatest in this Second Age of Martyrs, an inspired example to Christians everywhere, a light to those who love democracy. For is not the democratic process basically a Christian process—the more Christian, the more perfectly democratic? What other doctrine so firmly lays down the rights of the individual, the dignity of man, man's obligations to his fellow men, and to the State? Above all, man's obligations to God. . . .

Count O'Brien of Thomond, in his book, *Archbishop Stepinac, the Man and His Case*, writes:

"During the twelve years of his activity as Archbishop of Zagreb, he has accomplished many great things. But he has never before been so effective in his mission as he is today. . . . Today, in every country where free men live, his name is known and honoured and loved; his person considered the symbol of all the persecuted peoples in Eastern Europe." Among the newspaper circles in Croatia, he was known as a "sage and a saint"—one who gave most of his income to the poor.

It would seem, Saint Stephen, that your spirit, as vital today as it was two thousand years ago, had spanned the centuries and touched the soul of Stepinac. It is not only that your names are alike; that you were both born intellectuals who loved the poor and served them; not only that you were both persecuted for defending the Gospel of Christ, or that, subjected to an unfair trial, witnesses were bought to testify against you; nor even that, instead of "breaking" under the persecution, you both turned upon your accusers and in turn accused them, in unforgettable words of oratory and logic; nor even that you both were stoned. The great similarity lies in the "testimony" you gave to the Living God—that "witnessing" which is the mark of martyrs. . . .

There is one other similarity which perhaps only a woman would notice. I hope you will bear with me, Saint Stephen, if I mention it. The Acts would never have stated that "all . . . looking on him, saw his face as if it had been the face of an angel," unless you were, in truth, very handsome. Now Count O'Brien of Thomond, in his book on Archbishop Stepinac, relates that he is tall and slim; that "his lean face is not only handsome but really beautiful—of a beauty, however, that I have rarely seen." (Few of us have seen the beauty of angels!) "Yet his mouth and chin show him as a man of character, will power, and determination." Indeed, all his photographs testify to these facts.

For my part, I am one who believes that God bestows beauty for His own purposes. I'm sure that it drew many to your feet, Saint Stephen, as it has to the feet of Archbishop Stepinac. After all, how could either of you have escaped good looks? For the soul must perforce reflect its likeness on the countenance.

II

To Saint Maria Goretti,
Child-Martyr of Italy

concerning **SAINT AGNES**

Dear Little Maria:

If you were not so small (and yet so great), I would address you more formally, calling you by that highest title that man or woman can achieve, and which was yours unofficially before you had reached the age of twelve—the wondrous title of saint. Only a few months ago, only a scant forty-eight years after your death, was it ceremoniously bestowed by our holy Mother the Church; yet for all those forty-eight years you had been enshrined as a saint in the hearts of your countrymen. Maria Goretti, virgin and martyr!

What must it feel like, up there in Heaven, to know that millions here below now venerate you as a saint? Being so young, and so modest, the name must strike strangely upon your ear; and while I know that you listen, when you are called upon by the troubled ones of earth who seek your help, yet somehow I feel it must sound more natural to be addressed merely as "Maria"—you who are in time so near to us.

It is said that when you were upon earth you could neither read nor write. Yet seeing no longer "in a glass darkly, but now face to face," you will be able to read this letter even before it is written. There is so much to say!

First, I am consumed with curiosity to learn, if I can, something of the joy you must have felt when upon reaching

Heaven you found little Saint Agnes. I think it must have been Our Lady, your own beloved Madonna, to whom you clung through all vicissitudes when you were upon earth, who took you by the hand and led you to Agnes, because you are so particularly congenial, so strikingly alike. It must be wonderful, now at last to have found a companion, another small girl to play with—for when you were upon earth you had no friend; and so little time to play.

To be sure, there was your brother Angelo, your senior by a year or two; and there were the younger brothers and sisters: Alessandrino, Mariano, Ersilia, and Teresa. When you had a minute, you enjoyed playing with them; but most of your minutes were too busily spent looking after their needs; in cooking, washing, and mending for them almost as soon as you could hold a needle and barely reach the wash-tub.

How Saint Agnes must have welcomed you! I think that in Paradise there must be a special garden for child-martyrs, and that the flowers are very beautiful there; and that the winds of God play with particular gentleness through this garden. You two have much to talk about. And you are almost exactly the same age; which is a mystery in itself, since Agnes died more than fifteen hundred years before you were born.

Wasn't she pleased, for instance, when she heard you came from her own beloved land, that enchanted Italy? The cruel deaths you both suffered occurred almost in the same locality, hers in Rome itself, and yours at Ferriere di Conca in the Pontine Marshes, not more than a few hours' journey from Rome. You were only six years old when your parents moved there from your birthplace, and yet I'm sure you always remembered Corinaldo of the lovely poetic name—Corinaldo in the cloud-topped Apennines where your parents had met and married, and where you opened your eyes upon the world. I have never seen it, Maria; but one day I hope to go there as your friend, to come closer to you and to be caught by that enchantment which hangs over the old fortress towns which everywhere crown the hilltops of Italy. In one of these another saint I love was born—Francis of Assisi. So close to their turrets spreads the blue Italian sky, that in them one does not feel very far away from God.

In Corinaldo on October 16, 1890, when God sent you to your parents, there were two joyous hearts; and your mother particularly rejoiced that He had chosen the month of Our Lady—a fact you never forgot.

In these days, you must be telling Agnes much about those beloved parents: Assunta, who was your mother; and the dear father who went before you to Heaven, his name also holds the lilt of poetry—Luigi Goretti. In fact, your whole story is like a poem, although presented against the most tragic and foreboding of settings. An appalling poverty both overshadowed and glorified it. When the gay, brave young Luigi returned from military service to meet for the first time your virtuous mother, he had nothing to offer her in marriage but the living his two hands could wrest from the soil. On her part, her only dowry at nineteen was a picture of the Madonna, her own deep spirituality, and a fortitude of such degree that it struck all who looked into her strong, peasant face. Ever since she could remember, she had worked for a living. Love was the sole force to motivate that marriage.

When you were old enough to understand, they must have told you about the brother you never saw upon earth, their first-born who had died in infancy. Angelo, the next, you no doubt looked up to as a person of some importance, and like any little girl, of a certainty you were rather proud of this big brother. It was fitting that you should have been christened Maria Teresa, in honor of the Madonna for whom Assunta had such great devotion and to whom you were dedicated, and of Saint Teresa of the Child Jesus. Life at that time seemed to stretch long and happily before the little Maria Teresa, with her young parents eager to work, and with Assunta's courage capable of brushing away all obstacles. But, alas, one piece of misfortune after another at length forced Luigi to admit that he was unable to draw enough from the soil of Corinaldo to feed his family.

What an ill day it was, Maria, when he listened in his distress to the proposal of that fellow farmer who had cunningly devised a way in which he could make your father's strong muscles and kindly heart work for him! Better, far better for you all, had you never heard the name of Serenelli. And yet it was through that name that you came to your glorious martyrdom. . . .

Perhaps you were too small at that time to remember the details of the plan so cleverly worked out by Giovanni Serenelli. He had learned of an estate in the Pontine Marshes which had need of more tenant farmers. So having made arrangements with the agent, he persuaded your father to accompany him there. They would take up the land together as partners; but your poor father was soon to learn that Serenelli regarded him less as a partner than as his workman!

Serenelli had looked over your little family with a knowing eye. There was your active mother, skilled at cooking, and capable of washing for many; and there were the growing children, some of whom could soon be put to work in the fields. Two adults and five children—a likely lot, he thought. For himself, he magnanimously offered one son, Alessandro, his youngest child, motherless for many years; and who, while he could boast a little schooling, had been grossly neglected by his father and allowed to work among the rough sailors along the water front of Ancona, which lies near Corinaldo. A strange, silent boy who had been exposed to the filth of the world before his voice had changed. This abandoned one, now fourteen years old, he again picked up and offered as a helper. The ratio stood about four to two, with four Gorettis who could be counted on to work (he included you, at six) and even more as the years passed.

Once he had induced Luigi to remove his family from the high, wind-swept Corinaldo to the dank, unhealthy ground of the Selsi estate, it was not difficult to persuade him to accompany him to an even less attractive section of the Pontine Marshes where he had found he could lay hands on a larger plot of ground. It was on the estate of the Conte Mazzoleni. And that was how you came to live at Ferriere di Conca in the old red dairy barn, the top of which had been separated into rooms for tenant farmers. The awful part was that the gentle Goretti family were forced to share these primitive quarters with the two sinister Serenellis.

Do you recall that wherever you moved, the first thing your mother would place in the most prominent spot was the cherished Madonna she had carefully carried with her from Corinaldo? Fresh flowers from the fields always stood before it. How many a rosary was recited there! With Luigi and Assunta on their knees, and you children gathered confidently about them, even the irreligious Serenellis would sometimes join the group.

The life was primitive, poverty-stricken; but I think that you—Maria with the dark gold hair and the lovely child face—were quite unconscious of its destitution. To you, life seemed wonderful, and your father and mother like good angels. That dear patient father, you did love him deeply, Maria! I often think of you in those first years at Ferriere di Conca, and of how, when your father and big brother Angelo had gone off to the fields, you were ever at your mother's side, learning from her the household tasks, eager to assume all the duties she would permit. There were so many, you told yourself, too many for Mamma alone. To clean the rooms dwelt in by nine persons, to cook for nine, to wash and mend for nine, as well as to look after three very small children, was so monumental that even at six, you longed to lift some of the burden from those beloved shoulders.

All the time you moved at her side on those homely duties, she was also teaching you about Our Lord and His Blessed Mother—teaching you what was right and what was wrong; to shun sin as you would the plague; teaching you that it is better to die than to commit a mortal sin.

I think of you too, as such a small girl, doing errands for your mother, walking to a nearby village to buy the simple necessities she required. Not many years later you would be taking the doves your parents had raised, and the eggs from the hens, to market yourself, standing all day in the market place and at sunset happily carrying home a handful of coins.

It is related that by the time you were nine, you had become invaluable to the household; and while your mother sorrowed secretly that you could not be spared for school, you only rejoiced that at the end of a long day you could run to meet your father as he returned from the fields, and recount to him all that had been happening at home. Hand in hand you approached the old red dairy barn, your mother beaming a welcome from the landing at the top of the stone steps which ran up the outside of the building, the only access to the living quarters. (Mark that landing, little Maria! It is to play a sinister and horrible part in your story; and although you could not have known it then, I sometimes wonder if perhaps you may not have shivered, standing there for a moment, and pulled your worn shawl a little closer, in some unaccountable premonition of dread.)

And all the time, there was so little food. The good father

worked harder than ever, not sparing himself when that strange dizziness came upon him; brushing away impatiently that feeling of faintness. Poor Assunta, pausing in the midst of her heavy duties, would gaze out apprehensively at the fields, longing herself to take a hand there, that her children might have the more to eat.

Finally came the day of the great sorrow. As your mother prepared a lunch to carry out to your father at his work, do you remember how you suddenly felt impelled to go with her? As sensitive a child as you were surely had premonitions. You insisted so much, that your mother finally consented and let you carry the basket. Then, as you two threaded the wet fields, suddenly you saw Luigi, not with a sturdy grip on the plow as usual, but huddled on a mound of earth. Your heart felt as though it would break, as you and your mother helped him home and to the bed from which he would never rise. Within ten days the strong young father was dead, a victim of the dread diseases which regularly claimed their victims in the Pontine Marshes. You were only nine; and your mother was carrying the little sister yet to be born.

Now at least a part of you must have grown up very rapidly. Grief overwhelmed you; the heart that had been so light now felt leaden within you, as you contemplated a world in which adult duties were so clearly marked for the child of nine. In her uncontrollable sorrow, your mother must be comforted and sustained. You must help her bear the even greater material anxieties now confronting her. You must lift more burdens from her broad shoulders which now were needed in the fields to take over Luigi's share of the work.

With his last breath, Luigi had counselled Assunta to take the children and return to Corinaldo. Ferriere di Conca had brought nothing but ill luck and bitter disappointment. He had learned to distrust the Serenellis. Perhaps he too had premonitions. Your mother must have talked over her predicament with you at night, after the other children had been put to bed, and the Serenellis, father and son, had retired to their room. How she longed to return to Corinaldo! But there was no money, and the bullying Giovanni Serenelli insisted that the Gorettis owed him money, that the debt must be worked off before they could think of departing. He even locked up the kitchen cupboard after every meal, limiting the Gorettis to the sparsest food, so that most of the time you and the other little ones went about with a gnawing hunger.

So poor Assunta remained, bearing her fatherless child, the little Teresa, and doing the heavy work of a man in the fields; with Angelo, not much more than eleven, at her side. You had indeed become the little mother of four, in addition to being cook, laundress, and seamstress for the grumbling Serenellis who, now that there was no longer a man in the family, drove Assunta and her brood as though they were slaves.

But somewhere in all that gloom, there flamed one bright and glorious light. It was your first Holy Communion, given you by the gentle hands of Father Signori who, alas, was so soon thereafter to give you your last. It was at the Church of the Annunciation, in Conca. The Passionist Fathers at Nettuno had helped to prepare you. That day in May, 1902, was a wondrous day for a little girl who from the cradle had learned to love Our Lord, and who, from all the accounts of mother, sisters and brothers, neighbors and priests—and yes, even the Serenellis—had never once offended Him!

Obedience? You never practiced anything else. Unselfishness? Everything that was given you by the country people who loved you was brought to the others at home—a piece of fruit here, a bit of candy there. Heaven knows you possessed nothing, nor desired anything, except to give to others, Maria. Faith and reverence? Your soul was full of them. Honesty? It would have been easier for you who had no schooling to work out a problem in geometry, than to have told a lie. Self-will? You knew no will save that of God and your parents. And purity? It shone from you as from an alabaster lamp—clear and beautiful.

In a few months, you would be twelve years old. The First Communion had added a new personal beauty. From the time you were a tiny thing, a natural grace and a certain inborn refinement had caused strangers to watch you with delight. So it is really no wonder, Maria, that the silent Alessandro, who was now nearing nineteen, began to look upon you with admiration.

Had he been a normal youth it would have been no more than admiration which, as you grew older, might have ripened into a pure love; you might have had your choice, whether or no to marry him. But he was far from normal; and the good, devoted Assunta who otherwise might have guarded you, was herself too wholesome to guess this.

It was distressing that so soon after that day in May, when your happiness knew no bounds, the horrible shadow began to haunt you, to follow your every step, to leap at you from sudden, dark corners—to send your heart into your throat in palpitating fear. Had you been less courageous, you would have told your mother. But had not Alessandro warned you that he would kill you, if you told? Something assured you he would fulfill the threat; and indeed you were right, Maria. For he was a killer. Even if you had not believed that, there was the desire to keep any added anxiety from Assunta who was carrying so many crosses; and there was also a maidenly shame at having unwittingly aroused sin in the soul of Alessandro. You would keep quiet. But you would fight off his attempts with every ounce of your strength. You would avoid him; if forced to see him, you would try to make him good.

Dear little Maria, you had never imagined there was such evil in the world. That there was, made your heart hurt as you went about the daily tasks.... "Dear God, why does there have to be anything so ugly? Why must there be sin, dear God? It is such an offense to You! It is more hideous than that horrible black snake I killed in the swamp, the other day.... Take it away, dear God! Dearest Madonna, help me!" ... You could not know that God had selected you to be a shining light of purity to all the world–and that to become this, you must suffer yet more.

You had avoided Alessandro all you could; yet twice had he caught you alone, twice made his horrible proposal, trying to win you by flattery and endearments. Twice you had repulsed him, telling him his soul would be lost if he persisted; and twice had he threatened to kill you if you told.

Then came that terrible day when the sun rose, hot and burnished on the steaming land, the day of the 5th of July, 1902. I shrink from recalling it, little Maria. Forgive me. I would not, except that its tortuous hours led you at length gloriously to Agnes in Paradise.

I think you must have arisen with a frightened heart that morning, feeling that something monstrous was going to happen.... "But Mamma must not know I have a single worry!" ... After the midday meal, off you saw her to the fields again, accompanied by Angelo; and as you watched with relief, the two Serenellis. All the children went along too, except you and the baby Teresa. Whenever you could see Alessandro's back disappearing from view, it was as though a great load were lifted. So you must have felt on this torrid afternoon as you finished the housework, and picked up a pile of mending. You would sit with it out on the landing, where your mother could see you from the fields, and where the baby could sleep on a quilt at your feet.

Perhaps the return of the older Serenelli, very soon after they had all left, reassured you. Probably you hoped he would stay just where he had dropped off to sleep, there in the shade below you at the foot of the steps. Certainly he did not awaken when Alessandro, whose approach you had not noticed, suddenly bounded up them. Heart leapt to throat again, as you tried to keep the needle steady. But he flew past you into the house without a word. You breathed once more. Out he ran again, a handkerchief in his hand, and down the steps into the storeroom below. Then up again, so fast that you did not notice the bulge in his shirt where he held the long, sharp knife which long before had been carefully sharpened and hidden in the storeroom. A handkerchief and a knife were what he needed—and you, alone.

Then, from the interior, came his voice. It sounded choked and strange.

"Maria, come in here!"

Somehow, breathless from fear, you managed to answer:

"Why? What do you want?"

"Come!" he commanded.

"Not unless you tell me what you want." Trembling, you had risen and were clinging to the stone parapet. There was no time to look out to the fields, to call your mother. In a flash he was upon you; had dragged you inside, into the kitchen; had kicked the door shut.

That terrible moment when you looked into his crazed eyes and saw the sharp knife wavering over your breast! Why didn't old Serenelli awaken from his sleep? Could he possibly have been a partner in the conspiracy? The accounts do not say; and all I can think of is the terror which must have shaken your soul as you struggled with Alessandro, beating him off, and crying to him that he would surely go to hell. He himself confessed later that you did not seem to be afraid of death, but only to be concerned with keeping your pure young body covered; and for the fate of his own distorted soul. "You will go to hell, you will go to hell!" you kept crying between anguished sobs. He used the handkerchief to gag you. You fought on. And so, since he could not have you, he stabbed you; not once but fourteen times, there in the blood-spattered kitchen of the old red dairy barn....

In Ferriere di Conca, they knew nothing of modern psychiatry; knew nothing of a certain diseased psychosis which, when prevented from fulfilling desire for a woman, turns so quickly to murder....

Now at last, out upon the landing, little Teresa awakened and began to cry. Now at last, did Assunta look up from her work in the fields and miss you. She wondered why you didn't answer the baby's cry.... Alessandro had fled from the poor little limp body on the kitchen floor, and had locked himself in his room.

What a mighty effort it was, dear brave Maria, to drag yourself across the kitchen floor; somehow to reach up to the latch, and feebly call out.... And so it was they found you.

Confusion—unutterable suffering—as they laid you on your bed. Neighbors clustered about; Assunta weeping and hysterical. Foot police, mounted police; the ambulance to Nettuno. It passed the mounted police guarding a shackled Alessandro. They had to guard him. The crowd was bent on killing him.... At last the cool, white bed where you were to die, after twenty hours of terrible suffering—twenty hours in which you could whisper courageously to the agonizing mother; could murmur your last confession; could again receive Our Lord.

It was the confession, dear Maria, which, perhaps more than anything else, so surely set the seal of the saint upon you. "I forgive Alessandro," you breathed. "I forgive him with all my heart; and I want him to be with me in Heaven."

Up there in the garden of child-martyrs, you must have told Agnes all this; and how well she must have understood it. For she, too, died for precisely the same cause, many centuries before; and she, too, had so gladly forgiven him whose rejected advances caused her cruel death....

And of course she has rejoiced with you over Alessandro's repentance, which came to him slowly there, during the years in prison. Because he was a minor, he escaped the death sentence, but for his terrible crime faced thirty long years of confinement. Long before they were over, he had sobbed out his heart to the Crucified One, had done all that he could to add to the glory of your name upon earth. For in the long years in prison, he, too, like most of Italy, had come to regard you as a saint. You must have been very happy on that day in Heaven when you learned he had been released from serving the last four years of his sentence, because of good behavior. He was forty-five years old. Surely your prayers had wrought a change in Alessandro! And your prayers too, I think, must have led him to that quiet garden of the Capuchin monastery near Ascoli Piceno, where now he is living out his life, serving the good monks.

He did not attend your glorious canonization in Rome in June, 1950. It would have been too much; his heart would have broken again for the thousandth time. But your beloved mother was there—Assunta, the living mother of a saint. Think of it! And some of your brothers and sisters as well; and even some of their children.

I'm also sure that it was your prayers which had made possible the return of your grief-stricken mother to the clear heights of Corinaldo, not long after she had seen her little eleven-year-old die, a martyr of our own time.... And I like to remember that the Passionist Fathers, who helped to prepare you for your First Communion, enshrined your body in their beautiful sanctuary of Our Lady of Grace, there at Nettuno where you died. And that it was a Passionist who was the postulator of your cause for canonization. . . . The Passionists are my own special friends, Maria.

And so the winds of God blow sweetly through the garden where the child-martyrs play in Paradise. There, Agnes must have told you all her own story. How fascinating must be her accounts of early Rome as she remembers it when she was a little girl in the reign of the Emperor Diocletian. The Eternal City is ever beautiful, but it must have been unusually so as Agnes remembers it, with the uniformly classic architecture which Rome had borrowed from the Greeks, and the great white marble columns glistening against the bright blue sky. To set off their beauty further was the shining dark green of the poplars and ilex; and of course there were flowers everywhere, tumbling riotously from the balconies, even as they do today. Agnes will have told you how the people wore simple, flowing garments, sometimes of rich texture and color, and of how jewels blazed on the arms and about the necks of the rich—for Rome was both very rich, and very poor.

I'm sure that Agnes must frequently have wept over the lot of the slaves, who sometimes lived in even more pitiable surroundings than you knew yourself, Maria, at Ferriere di Conca. But it is said that she herself lived in a home that was rich and luxurious, for she was the daughter of a Roman nobleman—a fact which, coupled with her beauty, was in the long run to make things even more difficult for her.

I wish I knew how it had come about that her parents were Christians; because most of the nobility were pagans and worshipped false gods. Only the slaves were predominantly Christian. It was as true then as it is today, that Our Lord loves to choose His friends among the poor, even as He chose you, Maria; and as He chose those first great friends, the Apostles, the leader of whom, Saint Peter, had brought Christianity to Rome. So it seems to me that the rich parents of Agnes were singularly favored by God when He bestowed upon them the priceless grace of faith.

However it came about, Agnes worshipped God in Rome exactly as you worshipped Him in the Pontine Marshes more than fifteen centuries later. Only, she had a more difficult time about it, for she and her parents had to worship Him in secret. Trouble waited for anyone who avowed Him publicly. This must have puzzled you, Maria, when you first heard it; for you had lived in a Christian land, and it would be hard for you to imagine any other. (Had you waited to be born a generation or so later, you would have known about Russia, and the Soviet-dominated countries which have reverted to pagan ideas, and you would have understood better.) Pagans always hate God; whenever they run a government, His Church suffers. So Agnes must have told you how the Roman emperors had tried to destroy Christianity, insisting that the people worship the ancient pagan gods; and even going so far as to recommend that they worship the emperors themselves as divine beings. The Christians hid themselves.

Are you not absorbed in her accounts of the catacombs; of how the Christians had secretly dug them out by night—down, down, deep into the earth under Rome, hollowing out chapels where Mass could be celebrated and the Sacraments received in safety, and where the dead could be given Christian burial? In these, Agnes and her parents worshipped.

So the emperors went on, urging people to worship them; or at best the images of the pagan deities they had enshrined in beautiful temples. But poor and cheap as it was, at least the Romans offered their people something, in the temples and the gods; whereas the Russians today can't even dig up a poor little old battered tin god. All they can offer their people for worship is a cold abstraction known as "the State."

Had your father been a farmer in a Soviet-governed land of today, you would have had even less to eat; for everything he raised would belong to the State, and precious little would be left for the hard-working farmer and his family. And, of course, with everybody working for *them*, our modern pagan dictators grow in power while the lot of their people is even worse than was that of the slaves of ancient Rome. In our day, millions have been forced to give over their children, their land, their money, their labor—worse, even, their freedom of conscience—to the dictators' god of State. Protests in the Name of Christ against these abuses have brought on the Second Age of Martyrdom in which we are living today.

I find it so much pleasanter, Maria, to think of the two small virgin-martyrs up there in the heavenly garden—you and Agnes. When Agnes made her First Communion secretly in the catacombs, she too took on a new and lovely beauty. And even as with you, it very soon brought on a great deal of trouble. But where you had only one tormentor, she had many; for there was not only her beauty but her wealth as well. By the time she was twelve, all the pagan young men of Rome wished to marry her. Twelve does indeed seem very young for marriage; but apparently in those days it was an acceptable age.

But Agnes had her own secret which of course she has told to you—that secret of her promise to belong completely to Christ. I think of her as among the first of that great and numerous sisterhood which through the Christian centuries has accepted but One Betrothed. And so, for her, marriage was not to be considered. If they had only let her alone! But she was too desirable, and they flocked to her parents with their importunities. I have often felt sympathy for those parents who also knew her secret. They must have realized that continued refusals of those who appeared to pagan Rome to be suitable husbands for her would eventually lead to suspicion, particularly when they had to keep repeating that she was already promised to Another.

By this time, too, the persecution of Diocletian was getting into its full stride, and they knew they would have to walk warily, even though they were important people in the capital. The Emperor had decreed the total destruction of Christianity. As today in Russia, Christian principles were not compatible with those of a totalitarian State. The dignity of the individual, the equality of all men, freedom of conscience, the rights of private property, protection of women, of orphans, of the sick and the aged—for all these Christian principles, Diocletian had a distinct distaste.

So he did very much the same sort of thing which Russia does today. He confiscated all Christian property (which he found he could nicely use himself); he destroyed all Christian sacred books, even as the Communists have totally destroyed the religious press in the areas they control. He destroyed any churches he could discover; and he killed by the wholesale all the priests and bishops he could lay his hands on. The Soviets must have chosen him as a model—for their pattern of persecution follows precisely the same lines.

And I wonder, Maria, throughout those terrible days, how little Agnes ever got enough to eat. For it is related that even the food sold in the market place was first sprinkled with water which had been used in the pagan sacrifices, that it might be rendered sacrilegious for a Christian table. Probably her parents did not dare venture forth, because at the door of every public building in Rome, soldiers were stationed who forced all who entered to offer incense to the gods. Refusal meant death. The prisons, it is said, were so full of Christians that there was no room left for thieves and murderers.

It's a relief to read that Diocletian's persecution was the last to befall the poor Christians of the Roman Empire—the last of a horrible series which had continued, off and on, for more than two centuries, ever since Peter and Paul had laid down their lives for Christ, in Rome, somewhere between the years A.D. 64 and 68. As is so frequently true of the last of a succession of scourges, it was the worst. The soil of the far-flung Roman Empire was drenched with the blood of martyrs.

And it was just at this time of fear and cruelty that her most persistent pagan suitor began to look with desire upon Agnes. I wonder if she did not feel the same frightened premonitions which had possessed you when Alessandro began his unwelcome attentions? The young man's paganism was a horror to her. But above all, there was the immutable fact of the pledge of her virginity to Christ.

Agnes will have told you whether this suitor was, as has been alleged, actually the son of Sempronius, the prefect. It seems quite likely that he was, for certainly the story reveals that his influence with the authorities was strong enough to outweigh any respect they might have felt for the position her family enjoyed in Rome. Of course, the young man began with fine words and promises, and presents of rich jewels. To his great surprise, Agnes would have none of him or of them. Was he not young, handsome, rich—and (he thought) very much in love? He simply could not understand the repeated assertion that she was already promised to Another; for he had by various means discouraged all other visible suitors. Agnes may even have been amused when she witnessed his desperate efforts to discover who was the mysterious Betrothed. One of the legends relates that when he found he could make no progress, he went home sulking, and went to bed sick because he couldn't have his way. And that being a spoiled lad, his father then took a hand; but to no avail. The costly gifts continued to be refused for the same reason: Agnes was promised to Another.

You will know better than I, Maria, how the pagan father and son at length discovered Who was the mysterious Betrothed. At least one historian, Pope Damasus, declared that Agnes herself voluntarily avowed her Christianity. It was he also who wrote tenderly of her youth, as "hurrying to her martyrdom from the lap of her mother." Other writers claim that the suitor set spies upon her and so, learning that she was a Christian, out of spite betrayed her to the authorities.

You must have shuddered, as I do, at the tale of what followed. The rejected young man, with self-pride aflame, determined, even as had Alessandro, to resort to force. But where Alessandro who could count on no assistance, and with only a knife and a handkerchief (alas, all he needed!) had to work swiftly, the suitor of Agnes had the imperial government on his side and could prolong his torture publicly and indefinitely. This he actually relished. He had no difficulty in causing the young maiden to be cast into prison; no trouble at all in having the slender wrists and ankles bound by heavy chains. Then it was that he came to the prison, thinking to enjoy himself as the rough guards threatened her with all the inhuman devices of torture which were common to the Roman jails. Surely now, she would weaken. Surely now, she would renounce Christianity, and promise to marry him.

One can imagine his fury when she laughed at the hideous instruments, and even begged to be put upon the rack. To die for her Betrothed—to "witness" for Him with her blood—she could think of no greater joy! And when they dragged her in chains before the pagan gods, and commanded her to pay them homage, she raised the arm of a little girl and made the Sign of the Cross over the blood-stained, idolatrous altars.

Then, as she must have confided to you, began the most horrible part of the torment, devised by the brute who claimed to love her. If she could not be induced to accept one man in marriage, she would be forced to accept many men, in shame. As Tertullian has put it: "The Christian maid was condemned rather to the lewd youth, than to the lion." Lions would surely have been preferable, Maria! But twelve-year-old little Agnes was dragged to a house of sin—that same ugly sin which had stricken your own young soul with such horror on those hot sultry days at Ferriere di Conca. And like you, she did not fear death, but only feared for her purity.

She must have told you how they had invited all the profligate young men of Rome; and to each who tried to win her, she made reply:

"It is an insult to my Betrothed to expect that I could favor any other. He that first chose me, His will I be. . . . You may stain your sword with my blood, but you will never be able to profane my body, consecrated to Christ."

It was then that, enraged, they stripped her of all her clothing. In terror and bitter shame she lifted her eyes and besought her Betrothed—and she will have told you how in her great need, that first beautiful miracle was then wrought. Suddenly down over the slim young body flowed her golden hair, so long and so profuse that at once she was covered with a golden cloak. Then even they, the most profligate young pagans of Rome, abashed by her shining purity and awed by this sign of divine protection, slunk away in shame. That is, all but one—the one who had brought disaster upon her. He was as mad to possess her as Alessandro had been to possess you. His eyes blazed with the same terrible fire you had seen in Alessandro's eyes on that hot July day in the old red dairy barn. And he crept, like that black snake you had killed in the swamp, nearer and nearer to Agnes. But again she prayed; and again her Betrothed answered. Just as the youth was about to seize her, he was suddenly flung to the floor by an unseen force; an overpowering pain quenched the fire in his eyes and struck them blind.

Frantically he cried out; desperately he groped along the floor with his hands. Guards ran hither and yon. The prefect came. All had become certain that Agnes was a witch. Trembling with fear, the prefect implored her to undo the spell, while the young man wept in penitence at her feet. And now it was, dear Maria, that she set the pattern that you yourself were instinctively to follow with your persecutor, sixteen hundred years later. Agnes knew as well as you had known, that as a result of her tormentor's wickedness, it would be only a matter of hours before she would die—and yet she stretched out her hands and forgave him. And as she did so, she prayed. "My True Betrothed," she pled, "restore his sight!"

Immediately the young man saw again—the second miracle by which Our Lord chose to show others how dear she was to Him. And now, whether the grateful suitor wished it or not, it was too late to stop the wheels of Diocletian's decree of torture and death to all Christians, for by this time the entire city was aroused. "Death, death, to the Christian witch!" cried the mob. They lit a great fire in the market place, and dragged Agnes there in her chains. In its midst they set her. "The witch must be burned to death!"

But her Beloved determined that yet many more pagans should witness His regard for her. So, to the amazement of all, the hot flames bent and tossed away from the little figure in their midst. That "Sister Fire," whom Saint Francis loved, obeyed the will of her Creator and spread her burning arms hungrily toward the torturers and the crowd. Screaming with pain, they leapt back; while Agnes remained unscathed.

And now the authorities, furious at their repeated failures, called in the executioner. Thwarted in destroying her chastity, thwarted in burning her to death, they would try, as a last resort, the sword. Agnes has told you how she prayed that it would soon come, that she might have that unsurpassable joy of "witnessing" for Christ–of giving that special "testimony" for her True Beloved.

"Executioner," she asked, "why waitest thou? Perish the body which draweth the admiration of eyes from which I shrink!"

But the executioner, with pity, and trembling at her youth, begged her to renounce Christianity and be saved. The small golden head shook its firm refusal, as it had shaken it repeatedly for days. How gladly she bared her slim throat to the sword! And this time, her Beloved took her home.

It is said that the executioner's arm trembled–for you see, like you Maria, she was so very young! Thus died the virgin-martyr, Saint Agnes–the child-nun who would have but one Lover.

When you were a little girl and going to Mass with your mother, Maria, you heard her name repeated in the Canon of the Mass in which for centuries she has been honored as a "witness." And if you did not know it then, at least now you know that the name "Agnes" means "pure"; and that pictures of her here on earth always show her with a lamb, signifying gentleness and purity. She had gentleness, it is true; but it was coupled with a strength to make men marvel, a strength that has put her on a very high pinnacle in the calendar of the Saints. You had the same sort of strength, the strength that prefers death to sin. Even the means of your martyrdom were alike: you died by the knife; she, by the sword.

So it is that I am certain that the virgin who died for purity in the year 304 was there to welcome her who died for purity in the year 1902. She was there to lead you into the garden of the child-martyrs in Paradise. And surely there you have found other companions, other little girls who gave the same "testimony." There would be, for instance, the young Saint Lucy; and Philomena, a royal maid of Greece who was wooed by the Emperor Diocletian himself, but who, like Agnes, had pledged herself to Christ; and the exquisite Saint Agatha; and the bravely chaste little Saint Dorothy, and the young bride, Cecilia, who would have but one Bridegroom....

As in a dream, dear Maria, I see that garden of the child-martyrs where the children are indistinguishable from the flowers. There you and Agnes walk, hand in hand, for she knows that you bravely repeated the Christ-lesson she had died to teach the youth of those early centuries; that you had repeated it, unimpaired, to the youth of our own time. You had suffered as she suffered, to retain the shining jewel of purity, so dear to Christ. And I know she is very glad to have you there in the garden of Paradise through which the winds of God play—little Saint Maria Goretti!

III

To Father Kolbe of Poland, Martyr of the Two Crowns

concerning THE FORTY MARTYRS OF SEBASTE

Dear Father Kolbe:

There's been a glamor to our meetings which is hard to shake off, a haunting memory of beauty which has lingered ever since a certain summer day in 1950, only a scant nine years after your death, when we were introduced in what I dare call the most romantic spot in the world—the heaven-caressed Assisi of your own Saint Francis. It will remain with me, I think, forever. There we met in Italy—you of Poland and I of the United States.

In our meetings you have had much to say, while I have been silent these seven months, listening for your slightest whisper. Seven months is a long time for any woman to be silent. You who understand humanity so well will be the first to agree; and as a reward for such self-control will perhaps forgive me if I speak at last.

It was typical of Saint Francis when he learned I was looking for modern martyrs, that he should introduce you there in his own city, for in the space of a few months I had been in many cities—in Washington and New York, in Rome and other places. But Assisi was reserved for my first meeting with a modern Franciscan martyr.

You came to me there in the pages of a book, presented in the shadow of the great basilica where your leader lies entombed in the crypt beautiful, beneath the indescribable lower church with its dim vaulted vastness and candlelight; beneath the upper church where the frescoes of Giotto have since the fourteenth century, year in and year out, sent artists into a certain "divine madness."

The book was given me by one of your own brothers who like you, had determined early to follow Francis in this life—Francis, the true internationalist. Is he not Italian, and are you not a Pole, and is not the son of Francis who gave me the book, an American? Yet are you three all of one mind—the "Poverello" who died in 1226, the Polish Franciscan who died in 1941, and my kind friend, Father Godfrey Wolf, of the Order of Friars Minor, Conventuals, who I sincerely hope is very much alive at this moment.

However, Saint Francis was not going to make our introduction too easy. The book, barely off the presses of Paris, was written in French. Now it had been many years since I had read in that language; nor was I traveling with a Larousse. So I put you aside (my apologies!) for a time, yet somehow I could not shake you off. For your memory was gilded with the radiance of Assisi—that antechamber of Paradise. Then, as though to prod my lazy brain, there came another romantic meeting with you, right here in New York, when one day I met a prince. I mean a real prince—and one who had actually known you in life! Surely you will never forget your friend, Prince Drucki Lubecki, who gave the land upon which you built the greatest modern printing establishment in all Poland? And as though Saint Francis could not do enough for me, with the prince was Father Marian whom you yourself had persuaded to become a Franciscan, and who was one of the chief editors of those publications whose circulation under your leadership rose to positively dizzy heights.

If you don't agree, Father Kolbe, that our meetings have been romantic, then you have no sense of romance.

Naturally, with this romantic aura about you, you were foredoomed some day to receive this letter. I hope you will take it with the same Franciscan patience with which you met the many trials that beset you here upon earth. You are a fascinating figure, Father Kolbe; and one destined, I fear, to receive many fan letters. It is whispered among those who know you, that one day perhaps you may be elevated to the highest honors of the altar. No one, we know, dare make such a prediction; yet we read recently that the process for your beatification by the Church is being advanced. For you who had a host of friends when you moved among men, have since your death made new friends of thousands. And if you will permit, Father, I wish to be one of these.

Never having been in Poland, I grew absorbed in the accounts of your boyhood there, and was struck (as everyone not born in a totally Catholic country must be struck) by the deeply religious atmosphere which permeated your childhood from the day you were born, January 7, 1894. I have thought of you in that simple home in Lodz where in an alcove, semi-hidden by a tall "wardrobe," a little shrine had been erected where stood a statuette of Our Lady of Czestochowa. Before it burned, no matter how sharp the poverty, a votive light enkindled faithfully with oil on at least three days a week.

It must have been your mother who had seen to that, for we are told that she was of a singular piety, and had hoped one day to become a religious. But that part of Poland had been conquered by Russia; and it would seem that even when *she* was young, the religious orders had been dispersed in the usual Russian manner. Reluctantly Maria Dabrowska had renounced her religious vocation, and had married Julius Kolbe.

She had borne him five sons of whom but three lived beyond infancy—Francis, yourself, and Joseph. Heroic mother she must have been, for apart from bringing up three lively boys and making a home for her family, she worked unceasingly to augment the starvation wages your virtuous father earned as a textile weaver. We even read that she kept a little store in the front of your home, selling simple household necessities. Finally, by dint of great privation, enough had been saved to send your older brother to school. It would seem that you, the second son, were destined to get along with the meager lessons in reading and writing your parents could give their two younger children, and to help with the household tasks while your mother was busy in the store. It is said that before you were ten, you had really become a splendid cook!

From all accounts, you were a very normal small boy, falling in and out of the normal mischief; accepting philosophically the little punitive whip of which your mother made good use; and even on occasion, when you had been naughty, gallantly presenting it to her and offering yourself as a victim. You loved nature, it is said, and amused yourself by planting little trees in the garden. How greatly I sympathize with your desire at that time, to own a pet! It is recounted that one day you went forth and secretly bought an egg which you brought home and placed under the hen, carefully instructing her to produce a baby chicken. History does not relate whether or no she obliged.

It was, in fact, these and similar imaginative undertakings which caused your mother to despair of your ever developing a serious thought; and the story goes that one day she was driven to lifting her eyes imploringly to Heaven while demanding of you in tragic tones:

"Raymond, Raymond, whatever will become of you?"

It proved to be one of those occasions which, often unconsciously on the part of parents, strike children with such compelling force as to leave an indelible impression. You began to ask yourself, what indeed was to become of you. It was a problem which hitherto had not bothered you. All of ten years old, you decided in your perplexity to go to one who would really know—to the lovely Lady enshrined there in the alcove behind the wardrobe.

Was it from this day, I wonder, Father Kolbe, that you and she became such great friends? Somehow I feel that it must have been, for we have your mother's word for it that Our Lady heard your prayer. She answered your question by posing another. And your mother might never have known, had you not from that day forward spent so much time in the alcove, had you not frequently emerged therefrom in tears. A great seriousness had suddenly come over the young Raymond, this liveliest of her sons. All the mischief came to an abrupt stop; and quite naturally she feared you were ill!

Like any good mother, she began her questioning. But Raymond was reluctant to speak. It was only upon her declaration that you were sinning by disobedience, a declaration which seemed for the first time to horrify you, that you agreed to tell. So you recounted haltingly that you had asked Our Lady what indeed was to become of you. You had asked her not alone in the alcove, but again in church. Finally one day you had seen her, there in church, smiling and offering you, in either hand, two crowns—one white and one red. She had asked which you preferred to receive: the white, which signified you would always lead a pure life; or the red, which signified you would die a martyr. And you, no less, had asked for both! . . . No one but your mother knew this story until many years later; and by then it had been amply proved that you had won both crowns, the white and the red. . . .

From that great day onward Our Lady took a hand in your

destiny. Otherwise how explain the matter of your education? Convinced that schooling would never be yours, there came the day when your ailing mother sent you to the pharmacist with a prescription in Latin which the doctor had ordered. We do not know why it was not written, why you had memorized it, Latin word for Latin word, but we do know that the pharmacist, that kindly Kotowski, was stricken almost speechless upon hearing a small boy of ten repeat so accurately the lengthy Latin prescription. When he questioned you about schooling and learned you had none, he was even more amazed; and then and there offered to teach you himself. He even promised that he would prepare you for the same examinations which your older brother who was attending school would take, at the end of the year.

Years later your mother described the abandonment of joy which possessed you, and how pleased they were to spare you for a few hours every day, to the pharmacist. What a helpful friend he was! He never once let you down, and proudly saw you through the examinations which, to the dismay of all, you passed brilliantly. Now that they knew they had a scholar in the family, Maria and Julius determined that you must be educated, no matter what the cost, and cheerfully assumed greater sacrifices. For under the hand of Russia, there was no such thing as free education in the Poland of 1904.

And as we study your life, Father Kolbe, we see that it was not for nothing that you literally "ate up" mathematics, the sciences, and technology. Our Lady's knight was later to put them to work for her in a manner that would amaze all Poland.

From the beginning, you seemed to win the friendship of the greatest: first, Our Lady; and now very soon thereafter, the "Poverello," the Little Poor Man of Assisi–the very same who brought about our romantic introduction there under those fabulously blue Italian skies. Francis came into your life when you were only thirteen, a brilliant young student who went one day with his older brother to hear, at the town of Pabianice, certain of the sons of Francis preach. That was all you needed. You were determined to become a Franciscan. Carried away by your enthusiasm, your brother also made application for entry into the seminary at Lvov; and that was how, early in 1907, your father came to conduct his two sons as far as Cracow, sending them on their way alone across the frontier and into Lvov–two young Polish boys who never before had left their native town....

I have followed you with sympathy through those years at the novitiate of Lvov, where under the kindlier and more religious hand of Austria, monasteries were allowed to flourish, to send their missionaries into Germany and Russia; and where you approached your decisive sixteenth year. This was the time when you must make the final decision, whether or no to be a priest. During those years of adolescence it appears that, accompanying brilliant achievements in science and mathematics, there had grown an attraction toward a different life: toward the life of a military strategist (for the blood of soldiers ran in your veins); or toward that of an inventor utilizing science for the betterment of mankind. That was indeed a strange drama, Father Kolbe, which resolved the question.

Having achieved sixteen, there came a day when you determined to go to the Father Provincial and declare that you would not continue. Almost, the world had won you–but for that timely ring at the visitors' bell of the monastery. Summoned to the parlor, what was your amazement to confront your mother there whom you had thought was far away in Poland. What a drama was then revealed! She recounted that following the departure of her two older sons for the seminary, the youngest, Joseph, had also decided to enter the religious life.... And that, with all their children in religion, the parents had decided to follow the same path which had long called to them both. Your father had joined the Franciscans at Cracow—and now she, your mother, had come to join the Benedictine Sisters at Lvov. That must have been quite an interview, Father Kolbe! It determined your vocation. No longer did the thrill of military strategy, or the triumph of scientific marvels, appeal. You flew to the Father Provincial and begged him to bestow upon you the simple habit of the Franciscans as fast as he could. . . . Our Lady was guarding her knight.

It is not revealed how or why you accepted the name of Maximilian—whether by your own choice or by direction—but from that time forward you ceased to be called Raymond. Meantime the achievements in scholarship had grown to such an extent that by 1912 your superiors decided that you should be among the few sent to study at the Gregorian College in Rome. It is strange to read, dear Father Kolbe, that you hesitated to accept this opportunity. There is a hint in the accounts that the prospect of a great city terrified you—that you feared you might lose there that white crown of purity Our Lady had promised. But holy obedience conquered; and at eighteen you set off for Rome, to find it was not nearly as dangerous a place as you had feared. And infinitely more beautiful than you had dreamed!

From the records, what comes out most strikingly of those years in Rome are the deepening of the dedication to the Immaculate Lady; the clutch of tuberculosis upon lungs made frail by overstudy; and the outbreak of the first World War in 1914—the very year when, at twenty, you took your final vows as a Franciscan. Each had a profound effect upon your life. The first seems to have been tied in a measure to the history of your Order which had defended the doctrine of the

Immaculate Conception for centuries before it had been pronounced a dogma of the Church.

The second, that coughing of blood, those violent hemorrhages, seemed only to strengthen a will of iron which refused to succumb to any physical frailty. It appears, dear Father Kolbe, that you simply ignored the dread illness, and determined to conquer it by serenely overlooking it. Thus, you kept the secret so successfully that even most of your superiors and fellow students never dreamed how ill you really were. That you continued to live in Rome, supposedly fatal for tuberculosis, was only another mark of the Immaculate One's protection. But the destroying disease was to rise again and again as the years passed—to put you out of the running for long months at a time, just when your plans were fructifying. Yet did it teach a silent patience and that exquisite humility which only the truly sick ever come fully to understand.

The third, the outbreak of the first World War, made only too clear man's tragic forgetfulness of the lessons of the Prince of Peace. How far the world had strayed from these since Peter, His first disciple, had witnessed to their truth with his blood, right there in Rome nineteen hundred years before! There was so much to do, you told yourself, in so short a span of time, as the cough shook you again and again, and you concealed the red stain upon your handkerchief.... If, through the Immaculate One, and guided by the way of Francis, you could only win men back to the heart of Christ! Not just a few men, but all men.

There had been that shocking demonstration of the Freemasons who had seen fit, on the occasion of their second centenary in 1917, to parade blasphemous signs right under the windows of the Vatican—an occasion which sent you flying to the Father Rector to ask permission to call personally on the Grand Master of the Freemasons so that you might convert him. You believed in going right to the top! To your great disappointment, the Father Rector thought the plan a bit premature; and suggested instead that you pray for the Grand Master's conversion–which, dedicated to holy obedience as you were, you forthwith set about doing without delay.

There were so many souls to convert. You were always finding them on the street, in trams, on trains, and to the amazement of your companions lost no time in accosting them with a child's disarming frankness and the irrefutable logic of a scholar. For then you were working toward your doctorate in philosophy. You loved everyone–even enemies–so why shouldn't they love you and listen to you? Many of them did. It began to be increasingly evident that few could resist the young Franciscan Conventual with the round face of a child and the deep intelligent eyes.

It was during those days, days of discovering how many there were, even in Rome, the heart of Christianity, who had repudiated Him, that you made your grand strategical plan of winning them all back to your Saviour. An organization was necessary, as strong as that of the Freemasons. You would form one under the protection of the Lady Immaculate. *She* would endow it with success. All the dreams of the military strategist which had previously been yours now were turned toward spiritual strategy–all the visions of the technological expert now embraced the utilization of the greatest modern inventions capable of implementing the conquest for Christ. Your organization would be called the Militia of the Immaculate. It would make its force felt by millions through the printed word broadcast from great modern presses. It would be a work of true Catholic Action, to reach out into the masses–"to endeavor to convert sinners and heretics, and to sanctify all under the protection of Mary Immaculate." It was quite a plan for a humble young Franciscan to formulate, vowed as he was to poverty, and at times seemingly coughing his life away.

What is so captivating about you, Father Kolbe, is that your plans were always on the grandiose scale. Little plans, small endeavors, had no place in your scheme. Was there not the whole world to conquer? *That,* you couldn't undertake on a microscopic plane. Only sometimes it was difficult to make your superiors understand. You had to be very, very patient, and never once offend against holy obedience.

The Militia of the Immaculate was organized in 1917, there in Rome: a group of seven dedicated to religion and to conquering the world for Christ through Mary. (And while you may not have been conscious of it, Father Kolbe, I am particularly enchanted to learn that it held its first meeting on my birthday, October 17. That fact may one day divert the attention of Saint Peter from a less promising connotation of the date.) Lacking a press, the first weapon was a medal—the Miraculous Medal. "I am the Immaculate Conception." Hundreds of these you carried in your pockets everywhere. Alas, dear Father Kolbe, I weep over the difficulties and discouragements of that first beginning, when shortly afterward two of the seven died, and you yourself were helplessly withdrawn from the fray by another particularly severe assault upon your lungs. But rather than defeating you, it seemed only to strengthen the resolve to make the Militia a potent force.

How you ever managed your studies at the same time, passing all examinations brilliantly and acknowledged by your professors as a genius in science and mathematics, and winning, *cum laude*, doctorates in philosophy and theology, is just one of the minor miracles of your life. You had time too, it is said, to help others who found their studies difficult and who flocked to you for tutelage.

But now I must make a confession, Father Maximilian. It is not all these wonderful things which most smite my soul with admiration; but rather one small point relative to those days in Rome and almost hidden in your biographies. It is the fact that, when the bell for rising rang early each morning through the cold, dark unheated rooms, you, it is related, were the first to jump out of bed—you, the sickest and the weakest. To one geared to my own particular metabolism, Father, it seems beyond nature. You have made me most uncomfortable by setting such an example.

Came the great day of your ordination—Rome, April 28, 1918—at the age of twenty-four. And I become fascinated with the story of the bargain made by the captain of the "Militia" at his first Mass, with Thérèse of Lisieux, whose cause for canonization was then being promoted. It is said that you promised her your constant prayers for her cause, *provided* she would take charge of all your future campaigns. You kept the pact, and so did she. Not much later, to the joy of everyone, she was declared a saint—and many were the "roses" she was to let fall across your path! You two had much in common; for you both possessed much in common with the Child Jesus.

One year later, with the war over, again you turned your face toward Poland. It was July of 1919. You had spent six long and significant years in Rome. I think, dear Father Kolbe, that you felt you were going home to die, for on your own admission the doctors had given you but three months to live. But it seems that as usual, you made light of it; for almost at once you were teaching as a professor in the Franciscan novitiate in Cracow. You had returned to an even more greatly impoverished Poland than you had known before. Four years of war had ravaged the land; hunger and misery walked everywhere; a gigantic inflation was prohibiting the bare necessities to the poor. Epidemics raged, and the ranks of religious were so depleted that every priest was called upon to do triple duty.

In the few months of grace accorded you, you told yourself that you must spare no effort to launch the Militia of the Immaculate in your native land. But how pathetic it is to read that the colleagues of your own homeland not only showed no interest, but even regarded you as a trifle mad. It was an impossible dream which this invalid and brilliant professor had brought home from Rome. They shrugged their shoulders and walked away. Where indeed would one find money in Poland to finance even a shred of the plan? Discouraged and overworked, toward the end of the year you were forced again to take to your bed, thinking that this was truly the end. We read sadly that no one visited you, so fearful were all of contracting the dread disease. Had they gone to your cell in the monastery, they would have found you lying on the poorest of cots in surroundings so bereft of comfort that they might have been chosen by Saint Francis himself. It was therefore a relief to read that a few weeks later your superiors had you transferred to a sanitarium at Zakopane. How long the months must have seemed, Father Kolbe, as the entire year of 1920 dragged itself to an end!

But it was in the sanitarium where you had been taken to die that, paradoxically, you began your great work in Poland. The truly sick listened to you, and begged, in the long hours of enforced rest, for counsel and spiritual guidance. Then was launched for those who could attend in wheel chairs, your first series of discourses. Among the listeners were several nonbelievers; so again you rose above the disease which racked your every motion, forgetting all else in winning souls for

Christ. The young captain of the Militia, then only twenty-six, made many conquests there in the pain-racked corridors of the hospital at Zakopane. You pursued your victims relentlessly, with the candor of a child and the subtle arguments of a philosopher, as you had pursued them in the streets and on the trams of Rome. Few, it is related, "escaped." For you, that year in the sanitarium was anything but lost, replete as it was with prayer and exhortation. And somehow miraculously, and to the amazement of the doctors, you grew better.

One may read between the lines your eager assurances at the end of twelve months that you felt quite able to return to your work in Cracow. Reluctantly permission was granted; but you were sent home definitely "tagged" as a patient and one not able to assume the full rigors of monastic life. I can imagine how you must have smiled inwardly, knowing full well that through the help of the Immaculate Lady, you would soon be embarked on labors so arduous as to make the good doctors' hair stand on end!

For it is related that refreshed from the long rest, you at once set about recruiting members for the Militia—not alone among the Franciscans, but from all groups who would listen. The first small group which gathered in the "Italian Room" of the monastery, grew so rapidly that soon they overflowed its confines. Soon something more than a mere meeting place seemed desirable. Your voice must reach those members who lived at a considerable distance from Cracow. Again you dreamed of a press, for what was actually needed now was a printed review.

Who was to pay for it? The superiors had no objection, provided you found the funds. So, like Saint Francis before you, you became a beggar. And to everyone's amazement you were able to collect from a few charitable souls just enough to cover the cost of one edition. What a thrill it must have been, Father Kolbe, as it has been for the editors of all time, to see your first edition in print! *The Knight of the Immaculate One* made its appearance in January of 1922. And I dare say that those who looked upon that first copy had not the slightest idea that the simple little sheet would eventually become the most widely read publication in all Poland. We are carried away with enthusiasm when we reflect that at the time you launched your review, the greatest publications in Poland were struggling to survive. Many had already gone down to an inglorious death. The world will one day know you as a martyr, but I hope it will not forget that you were also a great editor-publisher.

How can we pay proper tribute to one who did all the writing himself and also coped successfully with printers and their bills? I know of no other editor who can boast of having paid his printer through an actual miracle.

I'm thinking of the time when your second issue went to press. You found with dismay, as so many have found, that there was no money left to pay the printer. To you it appeared quite simple. All you had to do was to approach the altar of Our Lady after you had celebrated Mass. There, sure enough, at the foot of her statue, lay an envelope. Tremblingly you opened it. Inside was the exact amount in currency of the printer's bill. There was a note, too, in awkward misspelled writing: "For my dear mother, the Immaculate One." You (and the printer) drew a long breath.

But running true to form, the printer's bills became an increasing headache. The true publisher met the situation. You would buy your own press, and operate it yourself. (Here was a publisher with but one-quarter of a lung left to him!) The superiors made the habitual answer: "Permission granted, provided you can find the money." Poor Father

Kolbe! I know just how you felt. (It was, alas, too familiar a phrase in my own youth.)

It is good to read that it was an American priest who came to your rescue. A visitor to post-war Poland, he overheard some of your colleagues teasing you about the fantastic dream of buying a press. After they had all had their say, he quietly presented you with a hundred dollars. At that period of inflation, it happened to be almost a young fortune in Polish money.

With what joy you must have conducted the installation at the monastery of the second-hand press of ancient vintage you were able to acquire! What matter if it had seen better days? The young Franciscan who was a genius at mechanics and mathematics would make it work.

At first regarded as a noble addition to the monastic equipment, it is amusing to read that as soon as you set it working, the friars covered their ears and ran. Never before in those quiet purlieus had there been heard so diabolical a noise. The floors and the walls shook as you merrily operated the "old girl" by hand. This, decided your superiors, would never do. Somehow, you and the "old girl" must go. And while it was indeed true that the climate of Cracow was not the best in the world for a tuberculous patient, it was also true that away off in Grodno, a city of past glories, there was a monastery large and rambling enough to house the "old girl" without bringing the walls down about the friars' ears. Moreover, Grodno had an excellent climate. The new editor-publisher and his beloved press were packed off there without delay. One reads, dear Father Kolbe, that your heart was heavy at leaving Cracow; but I for one am sure you felt that any sacrifice was worth it, to hang on to that noisy old press which was making the Immaculate One better known.

Your labors at Grodno fill one with increasing amazement.

It was all right, they told you, to publish your paper, provided you first performed all the duties of a Franciscan. These included your breviary, daily devotions, hearing confessions, visiting the sick. But fortunately two of the brothers volunteered as helpers. They too must have had printer's ink in their veins, for it is related that they worked tirelessly to get the editions off the press, after performing their usual daily duties.

To your friends, the wonder was that you remained alive. Caught by your contagious enthusiasm, more brothers volunteered, and the editions grew. With a worsening economic situation, publications were failing on all sides of Poland. But the little blue review from Grodno met an increasing demand from a public hungry for the spiritual inspiration it afforded.

The five thousand copies which the "old lady" began to produce had grown to 12,000 in 1924; in 1925 to 30,000; and one year later, in 1926, to 45,000. Some time after that, you were to look back upon these figures and regard them as puny.

I find your enterprise as an editor amazing. Needing donations to continue the work and buy improvements, you simply kept publishing on the one hand letters from admiring readers; and on the other, pictures of the hard-working brothers at the monastery in Grodno. It was the pictures in conjunction with the quality of the review which drew in the donations. Not only donations, but vocations. Everybody wanted to become a Franciscan and work with Father Kolbe on *The Knight*. You had the true editor's "nose for news"—a vivid sense of the present and of what the people wanted to learn at the precise moment.

When the Holy Year of 1925 dawned, it seemed that a special effort should be made for the Lady Immaculate. You would toss off 12,000 copies of a sixty-page calendar in her honor. The superiors sighed. So did the brothers. But soon the latter were caught up in your fervor and were working the antiquated press harder than ever. And now the new Saint Thérèse of Lisieux kept her part of the pact made at your first Mass in Rome in 1918. For the calendar was a great success. Aspirants arrived by the hundreds. The skies rained down a perfect shower of roses upon Grodno. Doubled were both the number of brothers at the monastery and the circulation of *The Knight.* Now indeed was it time for the Father Provincial to pay the press a visit. He came, blessing you and it—and how pleased you must have been, Father Kolbe, when he requested membership for himself in the Militia of the Immaculate, and decreed that a special wing of the monastery should be given over to the work.

With such encouragement and your own vision, the thing to do was to buy not one new press, but several. It is said that no one ever quite knew how you managed such a gigantic financial undertaking; but the fact is that the "old lady" looked up one day and saw a dashing debutante at her elbow—nothing less than the latest in rotary presses! It was a shock for her and for others. It appears that at the same time you also acquired a wonderful Diesel motor. The poor owner hadn't a chance. To his surprise he found himself selling you the motor at a discount of thirty-five percent; coming to the monastery to install it himself; and going to confession for the first time in twenty years.

And now, as the circulation of the review mounted ever higher; as more members of the Militia became trained journalists and pressmen—now the disease claimed its own again. How sad was the relapse, Father Kolbe, which struck just when all your dreams were coming true. There was nothing for it but to obey the doctors. They looked upon you with severity. Had you not fooled them for more than six years? In 1919 they had given you but three months to live, and you had gone off and survived years of tremendous physical and intellectual effort. In no uncertain terms they ordered you back to the sanitarium at Zakopane. Others must take over your work. You were even forbidden to think about it. And so I believe, dear Father, that now you faced the hardest ordeal that had ever confronted you. . . .

Holy obedience, prayer and rest at length did their work; eventually after many months you returned again "from the dead." Almost to the terror of your superiors you descended upon Grodno with an accelerated zeal. It had been rather nice and peaceful while you were away. What would be next, they asked themselves. They did not have long to wait. For now, enter the Prince! The very same to whom I talked, here in New York, in my second charming encounter with you—Prince Drucki Lubecki. He has told me all, so you might as well face up to a review of the facts. There he was in Poland, never dreaming that in Grodno, in a remote Franciscan monastery, there was a publisher whose output had burst its monastic confines and who was now looking for land upon which to establish a veritable city of publishing.

Apparently, no sooner had you heard the news that he owned an estate near Warsaw than off you went to see him. He has told me himself of how he met for the first time, the youthful Franciscan with the childlike face and soft eyes behind which seemed to glow an unaccountable light. In the quiet words and actions he sensed a hidden force, and when you calmly asked him for a portion of his land, he found himself agreeing. He would show you himself the section he had in mind.

It was delightful to hear him recount with a reminiscent smile, that while many had looked with envy upon these fine pieces of land, you in effect politely turned your nose up at them. (Nothing was too good for the Lady Immaculate!) At length the tour brought you near a more valuable section, one which lay close to the railroad station. This, the Prince had determined to keep for himself. That's what he thought (he confided)—but it seems that you had a different idea. It was just the spot for your City of the Immaculate. Just the right place to erect buildings, install presses, and launch the publications on a fitting scale, with the nearby railroad available for transporting editions rapidly to the four quarters of the globe.

To Prince Lubecki's amazement, you signified this was the only section in which you were interested. He hadn't the slightest notion of giving it away—but suddenly to his surprise he found himself saying he would let you know. The Prince relates that you said nothing but only walked quietly to the edge of the property. He saw you reach down, and scooping away the earth, reverently plant in it a small statuette of Our Lady, your lips moving in prayer.

Prince Lubecki returned to his palace unaccountably troubled. He should not part with that piece. He didn't know what was the matter with him. His mind reverted to those hours spent with you when he had listened, in worldly scepticism, to your stupendous plans. Restlessly, he paced up and down. Something strange was happening to him. The next thing he knew, he was writing that the property was yours, as a gift.

He has confided that all through the transaction he felt a strange force working on him. It was true that he had been greatly struck by the obvious holiness of the applicant; by his clarity of thought and a vision so wide that it held him breathless as he listened to plans which seemed to hold the authentic ring of prophecy. But to envision an actual "printing-city," with its own power house, its great rotary presses, its monastery and novitiate, all to be created by a group of poor Franciscans—all this seemed to be utterly fantastic. You were a mad but delightful dreamer.

And then the strange force would grip him again. He was really having a very bad time of it until he finally succumbed. Little did he then dream that not only would he see the fantastic vision become a reality and a veritable city emerge from his farmland, but that the day would come, when having reached the ultimate in buildings and equipment, including an efficient modern post office, you would even begin to lay out a private airfield on the domain.

Other witnesses have related how you and the joyful brothers arrived almost at once, bag and baggage—the baggage consisting of giant presses and equipment, quickly housed in temporary buildings erected by the group. It was probably the happiest "construction gang" that ever went to work, there in November of 1927, with you ignoring doctors' orders and working might and main alongside the others. Neighboring peasants caught your enthusiasm and lent a hand, also bringing gifts of food to each tireless worker whom they addressed affectionately as "little brother." It is said that the people themselves named the new town, calling it "Niepokalanow"—the City of the Immaculate One. At first the workers lived in the crudest of shelters; rough barracks without floors.

Do you know the story, I wonder, of the arrival one day of a young man who wished to join the Order? He was greatly surprised to see nothing but these crude huts.

"Where is the monastery?" he inquired of a peasant.

"There," replied the peasant, pointing to the huts.

"That, a monastery?" he demanded, stupefied.

"But yes," declared the peasant, "and moreover they seem to be very happy in there. They sing all the time!" . . .

So had sung, long before, the "little brother" Francis of Assisi, in the midst of toil; so had he sung on his deathbed. The song of the holy Founder has been caught up and repeated by the long generations of Franciscans. Its echo seemed to come very sweetly from your own lips, Father, and never more poignantly or more like the voice of Francis than when it soared from you as you died slowly and painfully, there in the Nazi chamber of torture.... But many things were yet to transpire before that day, which was both infamous and glorious, dawned....

The startled young novice who could see no monastery, of course remained—after an interview with you. He was the first of many who came as the City of Niepokalanow spread rapidly from barracks to buildings. With the buildings grew the circulation of *The Knight*. The figures would dizzy any publisher: 50,000 in 1927; 81,000 in 1928; 117,500 in 1929; 292,750 in 1930; 432,000 in 1931; 700,000 in 1935—and in 1939 you had reached a million. *The Knight* was a monthly. As skilled a publisher as you, naturally was not going to stop at one publication. Soon a magazine for children had been launched. On its heels appeared a review published in Latin for the clergy of all nations. And following these in May of 1935, that fabulous daily newspaper, the *Little Journal*, which rapidly began to cut into the circulations of the long-established secular papers. You had become a threat to the greatest publishers in the land.

We are told how in consternation they watched the *Little Journal*, a better general newspaper than they were publishing (and sold for less) snatch their readers from under their noses. They observed your sound editorial substitutes for the secularism and leftist tendencies which had been allowed to control their publications. I have smiled over that message they furiously sent you. "It's all very well, this amazing circulation," they said, "but you would never be able to do it if you had to struggle as we do, with gigantic payrolls. After all, you Franciscans get all *your* work done for nothing." It is related that your naive reply was: "Well, why don't you do as we do?"

There was another secret to the success which they had not stumbled upon. Just before the *Little Journal* was launched, three hundred and twenty-seven brothers, your "staff," had prayed continuously for nine days and nights before the Blessed Sacrament.

It is related that three and a half hours of every day went to prayer and meditation; that all lived on the simplest fare, and went with meager clothing; that you would never accept a new garment for yourself unless there was a new garment for every member of the community. We are told that the only relaxation you permitted yourself was visiting the sick, among whom you were especially beloved. You knew too well what it was like to lie helpless for long dreary hours upon a sick-bed; and for your patients every comfort was provided. I have heard that you daily enjoined, in the language of Francis, "Brother Motor" and "Sister Rotary" to work well foı the sick and the poor.

It would appear that now, having won most of the readers in Poland, you were eager to win others in pagan lands. Japan especially drew you. The priest-publisher would turn missionary for a time; and would establish a Japanese edition of *The Knight*. And I find it amazing, Father Kolbe, that having arrived with four brothers at Nagasaki on April 24, 1930, you cabled Niepokalanow just one month later: "We are sending today our first issue. We have a press. Hail to the Immaculate One!"

The issue had come off an ancient hand press, entirely in Japanese—a language whose alphabet has 2,000 characters. Your translator, it is said, was a Japanese Methodist for whom you wrote the text sometimes in Latin, sometimes in Italian. Even after such punishment, you ended characteristically in converting him. For you, Japan was just a stepping-stone to the rest of the world which must be conquered for Christ; and you were already turning your eyes toward India—and yes, Russia. Not alone in the languages of these and Japanese would reviews be published; but also in Persian, in Turkish, in Arabic, and in Hebrew. But my dear Father Kolbe, what you needed was not one life. You needed nine!

Meantime, the rather slender one to which you clung was again giving signs of wearing out. But in spite of illness brought on by the oriental food; in spite of a serious foot infection which for a time prevented walking and even made it necessary for someone to support you when celebrating Mass, you carried on in Japan to the point of building a Franciscan foundation near Nagasaki—in the oddest spot. Everyone said you had lost your mind; that it was the worst possible situation. Not many years later they understood. And looking down from Heaven, you must, I think, have viewed with satisfaction this enterprise—for this, the "Garden of the Immaculate" as you had called it, was the only building in the entire environment to escape the destruction of the atom bomb. Within the "Garden" alone, no one perished. The unusual formation of the land had given it a natural protection.

As the cherry trees flourished in Japan, so did the review, and from it blossomed many converts, many novices. Two years after invading Japan, somehow you got yourself over to India, and seemed to be on the brink of a similar success there. But Europe, your homeland, was growing restless and fearful in the shadow of some unnamable disaster preparing to come upon it. Polish cooperation with your missions unaccountably lagged. Then in 1936 you were suddenly called home. Ill and worn out as you were, it was no wonder your superiors forbade a return to the East, even apart from the sense of foreboding which hung heavy on the European air.

As disappointed as you were that the spread of *The Knight* abroad in a dozen different languages had been halted, I think you must have been very glad to see the wonderful Niepokalanow again and to observe how well the work had been carried on by the faithful brothers and the priest-editors you had left in charge—among them the very same Father Marian who was present at my second romantic encounter with you. The circulation of the *Little Journal* of which he was the editor, had mounted steadily, with many daily editions and one on Sundays as well.

What a warm welcome you received! The brothers had need of you, to advise on this or that technical point, to calm their fears; above all, they needed those exquisite spiritual conferences. From you they had learned the value of silence and prayer. "How will you be able to hear the voice of God," you had asked them, "if you make so much noise? He speaks to you, but only in the silences." And on leaving off work for prayer, they heard your constant affirmation of "the inalienable rights of God upon our time."

God was speaking to you now, in the silences of Niepokalanow; and gently but prophetically, you began to speak to the others. It is related that during those days you predicted much which later befell. You warned of terrible persecutions to come, of punishment for sins of omission. "How many souls have we won for Christ? We should have won more!" ... What was God whispering? ... You would not be with them much longer; and ——! The heart within you leapt for joy. The brothers watched uncomprehendingly the happy smile which illumined your face as though candlelight were playing upon it.

Loving your own unto the end, one evening after supper, during the octave of the Epiphany, you called them about you —not to frighten them, not to alarm them. Only to leave with them your "testament." I can imagine how each one felt, Father Maximilian, as you reminded them smilingly that you would not be with them always; and that, as their "father," you wished to leave them the greatest thing you had, because you loved them so much—the secret of happiness.

"If you could only know the peace and happiness that is mine! The secret is very simple, my little children. It is merely this: Love the Immaculate Lady! Through her, you will attain to her Son and find all happiness."

One of the brothers has related that here you paused, as though hesitating with a deeper secret; as though on the verge of saying more, but yet held back. Eagerly they importuned for more, begging you to hold nothing in reserve. Then I can imagine, dear Father, how, hesitating in holy humility, you confided in a low voice: "Do you know why I am so wonderfully happy?" Then, in a whisper: "It is because I have been promised Heaven. Oh, please, my dear little children, love the Immaculate One!"

The brothers, with moist eyes, crowded about you wonderingly. "Tell us more, tell us more!" But it was difficult to speak further. Indeed, dear Father Maximilian, I think you found this revelation as difficult to make as you had found the revelation of the two crowns, the white and the red, which you had been forced to make to your mother long before. But then you remembered how you loved them, and now soon, you must leave them. So: "It happened to me while I was in Japan," you confided. "And now, little brothers, do not ask any more. I have betrayed a secret to give you strength in the time of ordeal which will come upon you. You will be discouraged. Then remember what I have said. Search only to know the will of God; and if you love the Immaculate One, she will reveal it to you." . . . And then, as you left them: "Tell no one what I have confided to you. Tell no one while I live!"

Even so, we feel that you had retained a portion of the secret for yourself. For how can one doubt, dear Father, that Our Lady had also promised you martyrdom—that red crown she had offered you long ago when as a little lad you had demanded: "What will become of me?" The white crown had been yours always—a life of purity. The red which you so eagerly desired would also soon be yours.

"One lives but once; one dies but once," you told the brothers. "What happiness, if we of the Militia of Our Lady can die the death of soldiers; if we can seal with our blood our love for Christ. It's the best I can wish for you, my little brothers. For it is what I ardently desire myself." You had not long to wait....

September, 1939—who will ever forget? "Hitler marches on Poland!" Who will ever forget how the stunned world, taking up arms to "defend" Poland, watched from afar her heroic self-defense? Watched her die, bleeding, under the heel of the Nazi boot while the world, aloof, was still arguing about how she could be saved. As the hordes advanced upon Warsaw, the superiors urged the brothers of Niepokalanow to fly to the south. But you, it is said, put up a special plea to remain. Someone must stay to defend "Brother Motor" and "Sister Rotary."

Then came the terrible bombardments, heavier with each hour. The City of the Immaculate lay but thirty miles from Warsaw. It seems as though I can hear you, vehemently urging the others to fly, to rejoin their families where possible; to get as far from the Germans as they could. As some hastened away, their good father blessed them. A devoted few insisted on remaining. Night after night, as the bombs rained down, you were everywhere, "counting your sheep." There were shelters, but it is said that you scarcely saw the inside of them, so busy were you counting heads between attacks.

It was on September 19th, we are told, that the first German motorcycles appeared at the monastery door and took over all of Niepokalanow. I can almost see the scene, as you and the few faithful brothers turned your backs upon the great printing-plant built by the sweat of your bodies, your tears, your song, and your prayers. Ah, it would be very useful to the Nazis!

The long train of prisoners, the jolting, hungry journey in the cattle car; finally, the prison camp at Amtitz. Ill and weary though you were, you urged the frightened brothers huddled about you to pray; and soon you had them even laughing. The Nazis did not know quite what to make of you, since you met every brutality with a smile and the offer of a Miraculous Medal! The quarters were filthy; you had no clothing save that on your back; the food was scanty. It is touching to read that somehow the little band of Franciscans managed to follow, to some extent, their rule of prayer and meditation.

Some of the others lived to tell how you gave away your small daily portion of bread; how you rose at night to throw your own coverlet over a shivering comrade. Our Lady must have been pleased with the brothers, for there came a respite on her own day, one they had always celebrated with great fervor. On December 8, the Feast of the Immaculate Conception, you were suddenly told you could return to Niepokalanow. But in your heart you knew it was only a temporary reprieve. . . .

There lay the beloved plant—pillaged and damaged, but miraculously not destroyed. Gradually, others filtered back from far and near. Under a changed order, subject to Nazi regulations, feeding yourselves with difficulty, and hurrying on endless errands of charity, a measure of existence was eked out. How all of you longed to hear the presses humming again! Well, you would try. You would ask permission. It took months, but finally it was granted. The last issue of *The Knight* ever to be published, and the last article you ever wrote, went to press on the same great feast day that had seen your "liberation"—exactly one year later to the day. We read with emotion that, in the midst of a world torn asunder by hate, you wrote upon a single topic: love. Every line gently laid bare the falsity of the Nazi philosophy.

Only two months later they came to take you finally. It was the Gestapo, commissioned to round up all leaders suspected of opposing the Nazi idea. And since you were pre-eminently the leader, you met them courteously at the door—hoping, I'm sure, dear Father Kolbe, that they would leave the others in peace. But the relentless dragnet also drew in four of your comrades. The tragedy opened in earnest.

The curtain unrolled upon the horrible prison of Pawiak, in Warsaw. The opening scene clearly indicated what would be the development of the tragedy. I am thinking of that day when the hungry, weakened prisoners were called for inspection. It seems that the sight of the rosary hanging from your waist, infuriated the Nazi officer. Tearing it from you, he held up the crucifix, demanding: "Imbecile, do you believe in that?" Upon each of your firm affirmations, he struck you. But each time you were knocked down, you got up and repeated your belief. When he had finally beaten you unconscious, the blood pouring from mouth and ears, contemptuously he left you, a huddled heap there upon the floor.

It is touching to read that twenty of the brothers, left behind at Niepokalanow, upon hearing this offered themselves as hostages to the Germans if they would set their beloved "father" free. They wept with sorrow when their offer was refused. How gladly they hastened to fill the simple requests you sent: for a few handkerchiefs, a toothbrush, and a garment or two. And they wept again when they read your last letter, enjoining them fervently to go forth and save souls.

The tragedy expanded. You were marked for the next convoy to the infamous concentration camp of Auschwitz; the same where more than 5,000,000 prisoners were tortured and died; the same where the "crematories" of living beings smoked night and day. At first it was so cold that no sleep was possible. Daily, men died of hunger. The first targets were the hapless Jews. Next on the list for "liquidation," were the priests. Working toward its climax, the tragedy wrote in the role of "Krott the Bloody," the officer in charge of your company. Witnesses have related that, seeing your physical frailty, he amused himself by forcing you to carry the heaviest of the logs, and when you fell, by kicking you until you arose again.

After one such day, the story goes, he beat you with fifty strokes, and threw you into a ditch, leaving you for dead. But the red crown was yet to be withheld for a time. The frightened brothers dared not come for you until the end of the day. There in the evening they found you, still breathing. There was some sort of dreadful "hospital" to which you were carried, and where, it is said, you chose the worst bed because from it you could better watch the dead being carried out and pray for them. Secretly at night, the battered Franciscan priest heard the confessions of the dying; comforted all. Throughout the long ordeal of Auschwitz, it would seem, dear Father, that you gave your own portion of bread to others; that you forgot the sufferings of your own poor body in attempting to solace others.

The last act of the tragedy opened in Block Number 14, to which you were transferred as soon as able to walk. You will remember that it was toward the end of July of 1941 when the crisis began to unfold. That was the night the prisoner escaped from Block Number 14. Terrified, the remaining prisoners huddled together. Well they knew the rule: for every man who escaped, twenty must die. Each shivered and wondered. Would *he* be among the twenty? Some who survived have told us that you moved calmly from group to group. "My poor little one, are you afraid? Do not be afraid! Death is not frightening."

Many times you had faced him, Father Maximilian. Death was no stranger. Sometimes he had walked toward you down the white corridors of the sanitarium at Zakopane. Again you had felt his touch upon your shoulder in Japan. More recently here at Auschwitz you had seen him face to face, as you lay bleeding in that ditch. No, you were not afraid, but exultant. You sought Death as only the true martyr seeks him—to enable you to "witness" with your blood, to the Divinity of Christ. And now at last the red crown seemed to be almost within your grasp.

Moving toward its climax, the tragedy set a stark scene for the following day. A blistering July sun beat down upon the parade ground as the members of Block Number 14 waited, standing at attention, throughout the long hours from early morning until sunset—waited to learn who among them would be marked for death. Here was, in strong relief, that essential of great tragedy, suspense.

Men who had defied God, prayed for the first time; prayed with all their souls. As in the old melodramas, young men thought of their mothers, their sweethearts. Older men thought of their wives, their children. All men thought of their sins. "Could I but have a chance to go back; to try again! It would be different!" The pitiless sun beat down upon the uncovered heads. Silence, broken by sobs, and the shout of a guard; the commotion as one here, one there, in the long ranks dropped, fainting, to the ground and was carried off to be dumped like so much refuse upon a mounting pile of semi-dead men. For the day must run its course; the suspense must be attenuated until all the other prisoners should return from their work to witness the horrible example of what happened to a block, when one man *dared* to escape!

The testimony of the witnesses is scarcely credible, Father Kolbe, and yet they all agree. They declare that as those to the left of you, to the right of you—younger men, stronger men—dropped under the ordeal, you remained standing! They did not understand; but now, we do. Did you not see the red crown approaching nearer and nearer? Was that not enough to keep a man who had desired it all his life, erect?

Finally came the merciful sunset. The audience commandeered by one Fritsch, the commandant of the camp, had assembled in ranks about the tragic Block 14. At last, in a hush, the "great man" himself arrived, and inspected the ranks from block to block. As would a famous tragedian, he toyed with the suspense. Finally he stopped before Block Number 14.

"The escaped man has not been found. As a reprisal, ten of you must die. You will die in the Bunker of Hunger. The next time a man escapes from Auschwitz, twenty will die!"

A sigh arose and brushed through the ranks as a wind would blow through the cypress trees of a cemetery. All knew the Bunker of Hunger. Had they not at times been forced to pass it unwillingly? To hasten their steps as they heard the mad shrieking, the foul imprecations coming from the poor sufferers entombed within? No food; no water—no egress. Only death, as week by week, the body shriveled away. A valuable scientific test for the Nazis. They must ascertain how long the average man could survive without food and drink. And the Bunker of Hunger was their laboratory.

Each man of Block Number 14 bore a number. Whose number would be called? The Franciscan priest was Number 16670. And Fritsch, to the end playing true to Shakespearian tragedy, now introduced, as though to lighten the suspense, a note of comedy. Passing down the ranks, he asked each man to open his mouth and display his teeth! I'm sure I don't know why he did that, Father Kolbe–unless to make a sinister selection of those who had gold fillings. He may have told himself that the gold would come in handy, later on. However it was, when it came to announcing the *un*lucky numbers, we do know that yours was not among them....

Dear Father Kolbe, one tries in vain to capture the turn of your own thoughts at that moment. Was there not a certain, automatic human relief on that first instant of being passed over? If so, it could only have been an instant. For at once you were conscious of a stricken soul at your side; one who wept and sobbed piteously, one who cried out despairingly the names of wife and children. He would never see them again! Who would support them? Who would protect and care for them? The tragedy had moved from the Elizabethan, to the Greek stage.

Then I think, dear Father, that the red crown which but a moment before had seemed to dissolve before your gaze, now assumed shape again, coming closer and closer–red of such a beauty as to make you gasp....

Living witnesses have related the great tragedy's climax. Suddenly from the ranks, they declare, an emaciated Franciscan priest detached himself and ran, stumbling in haste, to the fore–right up, face to face, with Commandant Fritsch! You appeared to be pleading with him. Such effrontery, from a prisoner! Wonder you weren't shot down, then and there.

A whisper rippled through the ranks; this time like the perfumed breath of spring across the turquoise of an Italian lake. "He's begging to take the place of the young Polish officer—he with the wife and children. He's pleading: 'Kill me! I'm old and sick. No use to you. I'm a priest. No use to you. Spare him! He's young and strong. He can serve you! I'm old!' " (Old? Why, you were only forty-seven, Father Kolbe!)

No actor in the world could portray the surprise upon the face of Commandant Fritsch. But living witnesses saw it, and have given testimony of it. He gazed at you speechless, open-mouthed, as though you were a madman. But it was your clever argument which won him, Father Maximilian. You were of no use to the Nazis; that was obvious. But the younger, stronger man might be. The trembling ranks saw the Commandant acquiesce—saw one number stricken from the list, and another inserted. It was Number 16670. The red crown was within your grasp.

"Love the Lord thy God, with thy whole heart, and thy neighbor as thyself." But this was loving your neighbor *better* than yourself. This was the martyrdom of desire carried to its ultimate, into the martyrdom of blood. This was, to my mind at least, one of the greatest dramas ever enacted. And the hero, the son of a poor weaver, was a simple Franciscan, a follower of Francis, the little poor man of Assisi—one whom Francis, it is sure, would hail on his homecoming, as "my beloved son."...

What interests me most, Father Maximilian, is that the frail, emaciated figure, who had broken ranks and run forward to plead for death, was not the doctor of philosophy, the doctor of theology, who had won all the honors of high scholarship. Nor was it the scientific genius who had created from almost nothing the greatest press in all Poland. This figure who by sheer force of will power had many times cheated death of its prey—this slight figure was at the last none of these great men, but only a simple son of Francis who had been led to the foot of the Cross by the hand of the Lady Immaculate, the mother of the Crucified. Her hand had pointed to her Son, Who, with love, had laid down His life for His brethren. Through the years, it had become as clear as that to you. And that was why your feet flew so fast that there was no time for the startled guards to stop you.

Nor was there time, in the split seconds which followed, for the stupefied young Polish officer who had been literally snatched from the jaws of death, to thank you. For the tragedy now moved rapidly toward its finale, as you and the others, those poor unfortunates, were marched off summarily to that particularly horrible death chamber, the Bunker of Hunger.

When the implacable door had swung shut, it became immediately apparent that a strange change had come over the Bunker of Hunger. No longer did prisoners attempt every ruse to bypass its sinister walls; no longer did the Nazi guards themselves avoid its environs. For instead of the customary imprecations and madmen's shrieks which ordinarily issued from it, now there came forth only singing and prayer and merriment.

The son of Francis had carried peace to all within. "Behold, I am with you all days..." A father in a twofold sense was with them—one to comfort and console; one to hear their last confessions and absolve them; one to utter the prayers for the dying as they breathed their last. Why should they fear? All was well in the Bunker of Hunger at Auschwitz. So they raised their voices with Father Maximilian in the praises of God. The song of Francis emanated from the Bunker of Death.

Somehow they must have known that although you were

the weakest, you would stay the longest, stay until the last man of them had gone. You must have prayed to remain until they no longer had need of you.

So throughout fifteen long days and nights, the curtain of tragedy slowly descended upon the Bunker of Hunger. The voices of prayer and song grew weaker and weaker; fewer in number. Finally only one voice remained. The Nazi guards knew perfectly well whose it was. It was the voice of "that mad Franciscan." At length, that voice too was hushed. It is officially recorded that it became stilled on the fourteenth of August, 1941. That, as we know, was the eve of the feast of the Assumption of the Immaculate One. Upon that day, they unsealed the horrible door. There was the mad Franciscan, sitting against the wall with his head thrown back, a radiant smile on his face; unconscious but still breathing. And as they watched, the breathing ceased. They did not see the brilliantly jewelled red crown–but now we see it very plainly. The nine companions, brothers whom you had loved "unto the end," had gone on before.

The guards were shaken. Never had they witnessed anything like this. Even the Nazi officers, commissioned to make out the scientific report on how men die under hunger and thirst, had no taste for it.

The story has come to us from the guards, and from a few of the prisoners who survived that hell of Auschwitz–and especially from the young Polish officer for whom you gave your life and who lived to rejoin his wife and children....

To think, Father, that I might never have learned it, if Saint Francis had not taken a hand, there in Assisi; if I hadn't met Father Wolf; if I hadn't met the prince and Father Marian! And through them, you. The curtain had rung down on tragedy, and risen again for the world, upon romance. And now I pray that many will come to share that romance with me....

It was an odd thing, Father Maximilian, that when I came to search the lives of the great, early Christian martyrs to find among them one who had died both because of proclaiming Christ fearlessly, and because of sacrificing his life for another, I found a soldier. You were captain of Militia on the spiritual front; and he was captain of the guard on a military front. Leaders, both; and yet each possessing an exquisite simplicity. Indeed, dear Father, he was of such simplicity that we do not even know his name. Yet is he honored by the Church as a true martyr—one of the glorious Forty Martyrs of Sebaste, familiarly known as the "Forty Martyrs on Ice." And while in an old account, I found a list of forty names, there was nothing to indicate the precise name of the humble captain of the guard who was the greatest hero of that adventure. He could have been any one of the forty; but since he was most like you, I cannot close this letter without reminding you of him.

Yet I must confess that when I first heard of the "Forty Martyrs on Ice," such was my ignorance that I did not even know in what country it was they met their death. Sebaste, I discovered, was a place in ancient Cappadocia; and the ice on which the heroic forty perished had covered a nearby lake. It was the year A.D. 320, and the winter was bitterly cold.

Now while our captain of the guard was of great humility, he belonged to a very proud Roman legion—I found to my delight that it was known as the "Thundering Legion." This meant, of course, that its members were famous for their courage; and at least forty of them most certainly were. For when, during the persecution of the Emperor Licinius, the Roman governor of Cappadocia issued his edict to the Thundering Legion that all Christians must renounce their faith or die, forty men with one accord immediately left the ranks and avowed their Christianity.

One can imagine the irritation of the governor, Agricola, and also the puzzled manner in which their comrades looked at them. "Why put your neck right into the lion's mouth?" they must have wondered. "If you had only kept quiet, no one would ever have known!"

But like you, the forty wanted nothing more than to "witness" for Christ by their deaths. And in striking similarity to your own story, theirs is also closely interlinked with a vision of crowns.

You will remember that when the annoyed Agricola had put them all in prison, they prayed as one man that their ranks would stand unbroken; that all forty would remain steadfast and gladly meet death for the love of Christ. "It has pleased God to unite us forty brethren in one communion of faith and warfare; let us not part in life or death. Let us ask God to send us forty to our crowns together."

It struck Agricola, who had a fine sense of cruelty, that during this particularly bitter winter, a nice death to devise would be that of freezing. He determined that not a ray of warmth should penetrate; so he set the martyrdom for nightfall when in the growing dark, the winds of the Caucasus mountains would blow with increasing shrillness and piercing cold, across the lake. There would be no protection for the forty. They would be driven naked, out upon the ice. With an even finer sense of cruelty, he devised that on the shore, a nice warm fire should burn whose gleam would reach the sufferers. And he declared that any who during the ordeal would run to the fire for warmth would be considered to have renounced Christianity.

The odd part is, Father, that the particular hero of the occasion was not even one of the original forty! He was the pagan captain of the guard which had been set to watch the brave group and to see that none escaped. As he, warmly clad, walked up and down near the roaring fire he wondered, as the hours slipped by, at the courage of that small, naked band upon the ice. No cries of agony came from the dark, cold expanse—only prayers and singing. What manner of faith was this, that sent men to an agonizing death in such a spirit of joy? Not one had yet run, in apostasy, to the fire. And he could hear their repeated prayers that their ranks should remain unbroken.

It was then that the vision came. From the sky he saw angels approaching the lake; and each angel bore a gleaming crown. But as he watched the crowns as they were placed on the heads of the dying soldiers, he noticed that one was missing. In place of forty, there were only thirty-nine! And as he wondered, there at his feet he heard a sound and saw the one poor soul who had not been able to endure. Renouncing his faith, he had crawled abjectly to the fire.

Do you not find the rest of the story charming, Father Kolbe? "If thirty-nine men have such a faith as this, it must be the true faith," he reasoned. "And perhaps, if I hurry, I may keep their ranks unbroken. I will take the place of the fortieth, and may even win for myself that fortieth crown."

One can imagine his joyful haste, as he tore off his clothing and called to the other guards. "Tell the governor I died, proclaiming Christ," he cried. "Tell him I am one of the forty Christians of the Thundering Legion!" And off he sped to an icy death with the rest. So had forty gallant soldiers "testified" to Christ, on the cruel ice of that lake of Sebaste. And so had forty been brilliantly crowned.

Somehow, dear Father Maximilian, the nameless captain of the Roman camp, who replaced another marked for death more than sixteen hundred years before the Franciscan captain in the concentration camp did likewise, seems greatly to resemble you. The singular characteristic of his "witnessing" for Christ was the same. And to both had been granted the vision of the Crowns.

It seems significant too, that he died of the cold, while you died of hunger; and that cold and hunger are the two monsters which walk in the wake of war. Before you died, you had seen plenty of both in war-ravaged Poland. The human destinies of you and the great Martyr of Sebaste were closely linked with war. The forces which brought about the death of each, were similar. There was little difference between the Nazi ideology opposed as it was to every aspect of Christianity, and the ideology of the pagan Roman State. Christianity was a threat to the survival of both.

But what touches me most about your stories is that each of you had caught so surely the lesson of Him Who gave His life not for one, but for all; and in that aspect of the Great Sacrifice, you both imitated Him as closely as you could. From Calvary to Sebaste ran almost three hundred years; from Sebaste to Auschwitz, more than sixteen hundred—but the lesson had not changed. It held precisely the same force in the year A.D. 300 as it held in 1941; as it holds today. Nor has its glory dimmed.

IV

To Saint Ignatius of Antioch

concerning CARDINAL MINDSZENTY OF HUNGARY

Your Excellency:

It seems an unconscionable thing to disturb your peace, won so gloriously there in the arena at Rome almost nineteen centuries ago. To be sure, you've had quite a long rest since then. And I am encouraged by the thought that you are probably more tolerant of disturbers of the peace than others, for in your time, as a Bishop, you had to deal with so many! You may regard me then, as just another disturber, one of those who is forever saying: "I intend to take it up with the Bishop!" They belong to every age, even as they did to yours.

At this time, I've been urged by reasons beyond my control to implore the first martyrs, of whom you are one of the greatest, to befriend those of this Second Age of Martyrdom who have so closely patterned their lives and their courage upon yours. And it's not only because of your ecclesiastical position that I'm writing you; it's also because you are the only early martyr I have so far discovered who, with his fate definitely sealed, actually wrote down in advance what it feels like to be a martyr.

As I have studied your life, the more have you reminded me of a martyr of our own time, who yet has not seen death, but who has been walking in its dark shadow these past several years. He has been persecuted for the very principles for which you were persecuted; defied as you were defied; tortured as you were tortured (but yet with a diabolical new form of torture which destroys not the body alone but the mind, deforming the personality out of all semblance). He has been imprisoned as you were imprisoned—and like you, he too is a high dignitary of the Church. Joseph Cardinal Mindszenty, Prince Primate of Hungary and Archbishop of Esztergom, and Saint Ignatius, Bishop of Antioch, are as akin as brothers.

In small things and in great, you seem as one. The same love of God, the same devotion to flock and country, the same insistence upon ecclesiastical authority, the same quest for martyrdom, the same abhorrence of escape—all these unmistakably mark you both. An identical flame has enkindled the fire of your deeds and become a light to the world—yours of the first century, and his of the twentieth.

Yet even though he belongs to the twentieth century, I cannot write to him, as I can to you. The Communist jailers who hold him prisoner would never give him the letter. But Heaven is a "free country"—the freest of all, serene and totally immune from Soviet infiltration—and so I know I can write to you with perfect freedom and without fear of censorship.

Now if I were writing to Cardinal Mindszenty, I would try to comfort him in his suffering and imprisonment, and would remind him of you, and your similarity, one to the other. No doubt he would be shocked. A comparison of him to one of the greatest saints and martyrs of the Church would disturb him. But nevertheless I know he would draw solace from again reading your story.

I would remind him, for instance, he who himself is in the Apostolic succession, how directly you followed in that succession; how, in fact, you were consecrated bishop by the two greatest of the Apostles—even by Peter and by Paul. It's breathtaking, when one thinks of it, Saint Ignatius. To have known Saint Peter, to have known Saint Paul! By these, you were deemed worthy to become Bishop of the Church in Antioch which they themselves had established in those early tumultuous years closely following the Resurrection.

Antioch, a part of the Roman Empire, was what Paul said of Tarsus: It was "no mean city," being considered fit by the Emperors themselves as a place of sojourn. What a distinguished see you held! For Saint Peter had been its first bishop. Only one other had intervened between him and you—Evodius. And it was in Antioch that the followers of Christ were first named "Christians."

Certain books tell us that you were born in Syria, about the year A.D. 50, but I very much hope they are mistaken about the date, for I would like to think that it was actually earlier by some twenty years. I long to believe the tradition that you were the little child embraced in the arms of Jesus, as related in the Gospel of Saint Mark.

As you recall, the Master and His disciples had just passed through Galilee. "And they came to Capharnaum. And when they were in the house, He asked them: 'What did you treat of, in the way?' But they held their peace, for in the way they had disputed among themselves which of them should be the greatest. And sitting down, He called the Twelve, and saith to them: 'If any man desire to be first, he shall be the last of all, and the minister of all.' And taking a child, He set him in the midst of them. Whom, when He had embraced, He saith to them: 'Whosoever shall receive one such child as this in My name, receiveth Me. And whosoever shall receive Me, receiveth not Me, but Him that sent Me.' "

Please tell us that you were that child, Saint Ignatius! Almost you do, for in those wonderful letters you have left us, you wrote plainly of yourself: "Ignatius, who is also called Theophorus." Now scholars have a way of translating "Theophorus," as "God-bearer"—and while I dare not dispute them, yet if I like, I can quietly believe that it really means "one borne by God." (Sometimes it's very comforting not to be a scholar.) And while I'm sure you always bore the Lord Christ in your heart, I think it was because He had first lifted you up, when you were a little child. How indeed, could you ever forget *that*, dear Saint Ignatius? It was sufficient to sweeten a whole lifetime.

Certainly, something had sweetened it, had implanted in you that "desire to be last" which paradoxically resulted in your being first, as Bishop of Antioch, and which kept your heart always as humble as a child's. There was another factor, also. When you emerged from that childhood so loved by Our Lord, you became a disciple of His most beloved Apostle, Saint John, who kept throughout his life that same ideal of childhood as taught by the Master–and who, when a very old man and too feeble to walk, was carried about so that he might utter to the people his one, brief sermon: "Little children, love one another!" Perhaps, Saint Ignatius, you were even one of those who bore him in and out of the churches to give this one, all-important message.

With such a background, it is small wonder that you, in turn, drew thousands through love to the feet of Christ. And in this spirit, you continued to administer the see of Antioch for forty long years.

It is pleasant to reflect that you were one who made warm friends of the sort to stand by you through all adversity, sometimes at the risk of their own necks. The most important of these was Polycarp, who with you had been a disciple of Saint John, and who looked to you especially for guidance in his ministration of the Church in Smyrna, of which he was Bishop. He was indeed "loving Polycarp," as you called him–but I have a great affection also for that other, humbler friend, a fellow countryman and simple follower of yours, whose devotion led him to accompany you all the time you were in chains. When you were a prisoner of the Romans, he was at your side throughout the long journey across Asia Minor to meet your martyrdom in Rome. He stood by until the end. That was, of course, Rheus Agathopus, of whom you write: "an elect man who is following me from Syria, and has renounced this life." And I should love to know more about Alce, to whom you twice referred in your letters, as "a name very dear to me."

I'm so glad there were many others also—for indeed, Saint Ignatius, you had need of friends. Those alternating periods of peace and persecution so common to the early Church must have been very hard on the nerves of a good bishop. For example, everything seemed to be going along serenely; your Church was growing by leaps and bounds when suddenly the persecution of the Emperor Domitian hit you amidships, breaking in full fury upon the heads of the poor Christians in Antioch and all Syria. It was some time after the year 81, and was only to be ended by Domitian's death in the year 96. We have Father McSorley's word for it that Domitian, "a fanatical and depraved man, slaughtered numbers of the Roman aristocracy, and also ordered the execution of Christians who refused to pay him divine honor. . . . Saint John was banished to Patmos; and the Apocalypse refers to the 'blood of the martyrs of Jesus.' "

When you heard that he had banished your holy teacher, you must have breathed a sigh of relief that at least his life had been spared; but all the time apparently, you were inconsistently praying hard that you would be called upon to lay down your own! How you coveted martyrdom! Yet in the meantime, trying desperately to avert it from your beloved flock, though never at the cost of their Christian principles. When at last that old dog Domitian died, your feelings were mixed: relief for your flock; and inconsistently, regret for yourself that martyrdom had eluded you. But as you recall, peace was short-lived, for indifferent Nerva, the new Emperor, only reigned for fifteen months when Trajan, the soldier, took over.

It is related that Trajan, about the year 106 (the ninth of his reign), exulting from his military victories, determined to have the whole Empire united in one religion—worship of the Roman gods. He decreed that all who refused to offer sacrifice to these must die.

But as I see it, Saint Ignatius, he wasn't really concerned about religion. He was concerned about the State, which is a religion of sorts—very bad sorts, if you look at those today who follow it, like the Communists in Hungary who have made a martyr of Cardinal Mindszenty. Your early Roman Emperors were of the same ilk. Things are so much more comfortable for dictators if everyone in their domain believes exactly alike, worships exactly alike. Trajan was sure his laurel crown would fit with fewer pricks on the imperial brow, if slave and freedman were prevented from worshipping all sorts of strange, foreign deities, and would just settle down placidly to offering sacrifice to Jupiter and Diana. The Romans of your time had no more concept of democracy with its freedom of worship than have the Communists today (although these are forever prating about "democratic processes"). But bad as they both were and are, I think of the two, the Romans were more reasonable about the matter.

So Trajan pushed up his laurel wreath to scratch his head for a moment. He had just recalled that this strange sect of Christianity, which had suddenly flowed out of the East and was flooding certain parts of his Empire, taught that all men are equal. Horrible thought! Suppose the slaves should begin to believe it? Settling the laurels again more firmly on his head, he set off for Antioch, whence a report had come that one Ignatius, whose followers had given him the curious title of "Bishop," was leading the people there away from the State religion. As for you, I suppose you were actually pleased when you heard he was in town. Perhaps he could be induced to do what Domitian had failed to do—put you to death as a "witness" for Christ.

Tradition tells us that he interviewed you personally, and that you unhesitatingly and joyously proclaimed Jesus Christ as the Son of the Living and Only God.

Trajan knew that your exhortations had kept a multitude from obeying his edict—so under the circumstances, there wasn't much he could do but order you put in chains. Because of your sanctity, you may have fancied the rest of it; but frankly, Saint Ignatius, I don't. To be ordered to the arena in Rome, there to be torn asunder by wild beasts as a happy spectacle for the people, makes my blood turn to ice. To say the least, he had a mordant sense of entertainment.

But *you* literally ran after martyrdom. And it was quite a long run, from Antioch to Rome. You couldn't get there fast enough. As for me, I'm very glad the journey took long enough to permit you to write those wonderful letters along the route—a priceless heritage of Christian tradition, handing down as they do the teaching of the Church, received by you directly from the Apostles, who in turn had received it from Our Lord. In them carefully is laid down the doctrine of the Virgin Birth, of the Holy Eucharist, of the Resurrection, of baptism—and most emphatically, the divine authority of the bishops. Clear as a mountain stream runs the doctrine, from that day to this, as taught unequivocally by a long succession of bishops of the Catholic Church; even as taught by His Eminence, Joseph Cardinal Mindszenty, Prince Primate of Hungary and Archbishop of Esztergom.

Eusebius, whom we have to thank for your story, relates that you wrote seven letters in all (though others have held there were more) while you were rushing headlong across Asia Minor toward that ghastly arena, bound by chains and guarded by Roman soldiers to whom you frankly referred as "ten leopards." The milder and more submissive you were, the more vicious and brutal were they. As you put it yourself: "Now I become the more a disciple, for their ill deeds. . . . I long for the beasts that are prepared for me." In your mind, those starved lions appeared tame in comparison to your custodians. Poor Saint Ignatius!

Curiously enough, the guards did not seem to object to your receiving visitors, and even delegations, along the route. Everywhere you passed, throngs of Christians came to you, some from long distances, for you were already a famous man in all the Empire; and to the Christians themselves, a beacon light. Bishops came; or if they could not, sent emissaries and persons to serve you, to carry your letters back and forth. Perhaps Rome thought that the more who saw your humiliation in chains, the better would be the example to all tempted to defy the imperial edict—yet I cannot but contrast this aspect of your treatment with the arrest of Cardinal Mindszenty. When they apprehended him, they took him away from his home on a dark December night, after they had made certain no one would see. Rome worked in the sunlight; the Communists do their ill deeds in the dark. But then, Rome was sure of its power, while the Communists are not.

So the Bishops' emissaries carried back to their churches those great letters—to the Ephesians, to the Magnesians, to the Trallians, to the Romans, to the Philadelphians, to the Smyrneans; and finally, to your beloved Polycarp. It is cause for wonder that you could write them, dear Saint Ignatius, considering the hardships you were suffering, and with those "ten leopards" kicking you about from morning until night!

What seems even worse to us was the ever-present vision of those hungry lions, their jaws agape, waiting for you. The nightmare of what was to come must have been horrible. Yet, paradoxically, you longed to reach Rome. And in the letters you sought comfort by repeating, with such beauty, the Christian doctrine: "And the virginity of Mary, and her giving birth, were hidden from the prince of this world, as was also the death of the Lord. Three mysteries of a cry which was wrought in the stillness of God."

Mainly, it seems, you were writing to strengthen the infant Church; to unify it under the authority of the Bishops—for repeatedly you exhort your readers to follow their Bishops implicitly. Of equal concern was that they should abjure all heresy; and finally, loving your own unto the end, you urged the other churches not to neglect your own beloved church in Antioch from which you had been so violently torn.

But it is your epistle to the Romans which thrills me beyond all! There speaks the true martyr, the "witness," the lover who understands that "greater love no man hath than this, that he lay down his life for his friend." Your one terror was that others might prevent you. Above all, the Roman Christians, who were waiting to welcome the great Bishop of Antioch—he who had known Peter, and Paul, and John. You knew that if they would, they had a fair chance of preventing your martyrdom, for among them were some who were close to the emperor.

All through the journey you were ridden by fear, lest at the last, you be cheated of the prize so coveted. And while I pity the passion of pleading which rings forth from that letter to the Romans, and which, like all passion, involved suffering, I cannot but be enchanted by its ardor.

First you wrote how you had long prayed to see them, these Christians of Rome; and then added naively: "I have obtained more than I asked..." (I'll say you had, when not only were you now to see them, but also to be eaten alive before their eyes!) And then, tumultuously, you poured forth this plea:

"For in bondage in Christ Jesus, I hope to greet you, if it be His will, and that I be found worthy to the end. For the beginning has been well ordered, if I may obtain grace to come unhindered to my lot. For I am afraid of your love, lest even that do me wrong. For it is easy for you to do what you will, but it is difficult for me to attain to God, if you do not spare me.... For neither shall I ever have such an opportunity of attaining to God; nor can you, if you be but silent, have any better deed ascribed to you.... Grant me nothing more than that I be poured out to God, while an altar is still ready....

"It is better for me to die in Christ Jesus than to be king over the ends of the earth....

"Only pray for me for strength, both inward and outward ... that I may not only be called a Christian, but also be found to be one.... I am writing to all the Churches ... that I am dying willingly for God's sake, if you do not hinder it. I beseech you, be not an 'unseasonable kindness' to me."

And here I find a delightful footnote, Saint Ignatius, in the translation of your letters by Kirsopp Lake, in *The Apostolic Fathers*; he notes that you may have been partially quoting a proverb of Zenobius to the effect that "an unseasonable kindness is nothing different from hostility." (While I don't know Zenobius at all, I certainly think he has something there.)

Then you faced up to the grim realism of the situation, as you must have met it many times during the journey, in the long, still watches of the night:

"Suffer me to be eaten by the beasts, through whom I can attain to God. I am the wheat of God, and let me be ground by the teeth of wild beasts that I may be found the pure bread of Christ. Rather entice the wild beasts that they may become my tomb, and leave no trace of my body, that when I fall asleep I be not burdensome to any.... Now I am learning in my bonds to give up all desires."

All but the desire of martyrdom. And of the seamy side of *that*, you had no illusions:

"I pray that the beasts may be found prompt for me. I will even entice them to devour me promptly; not as has happened to some whom they have not touched from fear; even if they be unwilling of themselves, I will force them to it. Grant me this favour.... Let there come on me fire, and cross, and struggles with wild beasts; cutting, and tearing asunder, rackings of bones, mangling of limbs, crushing of my whole body, cruel tortures of the devil—that I but attain to Jesus Christ!"

Well, after all that, the Roman Christians could do nothing but acquiesce. So when finally you arrived at the city gates, they came forth to greet you as a saint.

It is related that "great crowds assembled to receive the benediction of one who was practically already a martyr." Close to you must have stood those faithful friends who had come the long way with you. That brave, useful Burrhus, a deacon of Ephesus, who had acted as your scribe—and the others. The legend goes that it was on December 20th, the last day of the public games. You arrived just in time, it would seem, for Trajan to climax the games with his biggest and best "show."

There at last in the Coliseum, dear Saint Ignatius, in the year A.D. 108, was your long desire fulfilled. I'm sure you entered the arena with firm step, your head held high; the radiance of fulfillment on your face. There, before a tumultuous throng and weeping friends, as a triumphant "witness" you poured out your blood for Christ. It is told that two fierce lions played their part—swiftly, thank God.

And the faithful Rheus Agathopus remained until the end. It was he, and the deacon of Cilicia, Philo, whom you had called "a man of good report," who gathered up what remained of you, and carried the relics back to Antioch where they were interred outside the city gates, "not far from the beautiful suburb of Daphne." Eventually they were taken back to Rome, to rest in the Church of Saint Clement. And it was also these two friends who wrote the ancient story of your martyrdom. . . .

Although he has probably read it many times, it is of this story that I would remind Joseph Cardinal Mindszenty, were I able to reach him with a letter—believing it would comfort him in his long, living martyrdom.

As for his life, I'm wondering, Saint Ignatius, how much of it you have followed. Have you observed how, as Bishops, you both fought to maintain identical strongholds in your battle to preserve Christianity? Yet almost two thousand years separate you—you of Syria and he of Hungary. His paternal ancestors had emigrated to the land of the Magyars from Germany some three hundred years before he was born.

In those centuries, although the family continued to bear the German name of Pehm, they had become thoroughly Hungarian, devoted to the land, and to its deeply Christian character implanted a thousand years ago by the great king who became another Saint Stephen, and who derived his name from our first glorious Christian martyr. The Pehm who was to become a bishop, and then cardinal; who was to attain to that uniquely powerful title, peculiar to the deep-set Christianity of the sons of Stephen—the title of Prince Primate of

Hungary—was born of peasants whose forbears in past generations had received privileges from the crown.

Writers have described the lovely rural country about the little town of Cseh-Mindszent, the small and rather poor farm which had belonged to the Pehms for generations, and the house of sun-baked brick in which Joseph was born on March 29, 1892. It lies in the county of Vas, near the Austrian and Yugoslav borders. Joseph was one of six children in a family whose resources had been too slender to permit an older brother to study for the priesthood.

But what was lacking in material strength was there in abundance in spiritual force—in the strong, just characters of his father and mother, from whom Joseph learned his first lessons in honesty and fair play, and in the total love of God. From his father and brothers he also learned how to plant and to plough; how to swing a scythe; and it must be that long hours of work in the fields through many a harvest built up within him that singular endurance which later enabled him to labor so tirelessly, and at the end to withstand treatment which in all likelihood would have killed another.

With the other children of the village, he went to school when he was six—but he differed from the other children, and it soon became evident that here was a scholar. At least one account relates that when he was ten he attracted the attention of a person of some influence who, visiting Cseh-Mindszent, was struck by Joseph's intelligence and opened the way for arrangements to send him to the Latin high school in the city of Szombathely. It was the old Roman town of Sabaria which had been a part of the Empire when you, Saint Ignatius, were forced to bow to its decrees in far-off Antioch.

It is said that because of his poverty, great hardships attended his studies there. Yet he always managed to get himself home for the vacation periods, to see the mother to whom he was closer than to anyone else on earth; and to do his share in the fields at the side of his father.

It was in Szombathely that the Master you both followed, called to him silently; it was there he resolved to be a priest. It was also there that he entered upon his studies at the seminary; into the blissful peace of which in 1914 there broke thunderously the first World War. Local hospitals were soon crowded with war victims; even the seminary students were called upon to nurse the wounded. Joseph did triple duty, adding spiritual care of the sick to the task of nursing, and continuing his studies at the same time. While the war still raged he was ordained a priest, on June 12, 1915, and returned to his home in Cseh-Mindszent to offer his first Mass.

All of Cseh-Mindszent and the nearby communities turned out joyfully for the service, held in the open air because the church was too small to accommodate so large a gathering. It was a happy day of celebration, and particularly was his mother's cup of joy filled to the brim. When the Mass was finished, and all the congratulations said, and his friends departed, Joseph donned his working clothes and went out into the fields to help his father with the harvest.

The new priest's first assignment was as chaplain to a small church in Felsopaty; but not much more than a year later he was appointed to teach religion in the State high school at Zalaegerszeg, the county seat of Zala and a prominent town in western Hungary. During that first year of teaching in 1917, he wrote his book *Motherhood*, whose inspiration was from his own beloved mother. Rapidly the young priest was recognized as a scholar, and was soon to become the editor of a paper, *News of Zala County*.

It was in the columns of this journal that he began to cry out publicly against the Red terror which, upon the collapse of the Austro-Hungarian monarchy and the defeat of his country in 1918, began to stretch its long arm out from Russia and spread its fingers ravenously toward Hungary. Father Joseph was then only twenty-six years old; but by his voice in the classroom and his printed word, warnings were uttered unceasingly and without fear against the violence and disregard of human rights which marked the path of this new enemy.

When, more than thirty years later, he was tried and convicted by a Red court, they knew him well as an old and fearless foe who had never lost an opportunity to decry their fixed purpose: the destruction of Christianity, to be wrought by the deliberate tearing down of all the principles upon which Christianity is founded.

So came about his first imprisonment, in March, 1919. This was upon the rise of Bela Kun, Moscow-trained to sow revolution and overthrow the weak Karolyi government which had run the country in the name of the new Hungarian republic ever since the abdication of the King at the close of 1918. As distressing as was the arrest, I think you will be pleased, dear Saint Ignatius, that Father Joseph was on his way to pay a filial visit to his bishop, when the revolutionaries seized him. He was imprisoned in the Bishop's Castle in Szombathely; while the poor Bishop himself, Janos Mikes, was sent off to a prison cell in Budapest.

Father Joseph's first term of imprisonment lasted only two weeks, but upon his release he was strictly warned not to return to Zalaegerszeg. And that, of course, was the first thing he did! So immediately there was another arrest. He was taken back to Szombathely and reimprisoned; and when Bela Kun took over the government on March 21st, Father Joseph was held as hostage against any opposition to the new regime which might arise in western Hungary where he had taught and worked. If trouble began there, he would be hanged.

After more than three months in a horrible, pest-ridden jail, cheering as best he could his frightened companions, he was again released and sent back to Zalaegerszeg; again with a warning. He paid no more attention to this one than he had to the last. In fact, Saint Ignatius, warnings from the Reds had no more effect upon him than those of Trajan had upon you. Even as you, he delighted in doing precisely the opposite to what was recommended by the enemies of his Master. And the marvel of it is that right here at the start, he was not "liquidated." Later, when he had become Cardinal and Prince Primate, it was a different matter—but in 1919 he might have been disposed of, without much fuss.

Instead, however, of putting out of the way permanently this eloquent and persistent critic, they sent him back to his native village where they felt he could do the least harm. There in Cseh-Mindszent he was ordered to report regularly to the village directorate which the Reds had set up. Its members had been chosen from the local farmers as representatives of the proletariat, and they weren't any happier than was Father Joseph over Bela Kun—but they had been forced to serve. Luckily, they all turned out to be old friends of Father Joseph's. So he was left in peace. And he was home again, with his mother; home where he could say Mass daily in the little church; home where he could work long hours out of doors and spend much time thinking what he might do, what he could do, to save the country he loved so much.

Passing travelers brought word of wholesale murders and a reign of terror. Many of these were political refugees, fleeing for their lives and seeking to cross the frontier into Yugoslavia. At the Pehm farm they were refreshed and rested—and frequently Father Joseph himself would guide them across the border.

They all thought, so terrible was the reign of Bela Kun,

that it would last forever; but actually it only endured little more than four months. The wily peasants had stubbornly resisted collaboration, and when Budapest began to starve, Bela Kun saved his neck by fleeing to Vienna, relinquishing authority to a Socialist government. It was the summer of 1919.

For a brief moment the sun seemed to shine again upon Hungary. Bishop Mikes, after an escape from prison and a period in hiding, returned to his see at Szombathely, and Father Joseph went there to welcome him. Although they had been separated throughout the terror, they had become warmer friends; for the Bishop had been informed of Father Joseph's unflinching resistance. He knew also what a force he had been in preventing bloodshed upon the overthrow of Bela Kun when an angry populace would have done violence to those who had supported the regime.

It was fitting then, that Father Joseph, who was not yet twenty-eight years old, should be made administrator in Zalaegerszeg where first he had thrown his lance against the philosophy of Moscow. Very soon thereafter he was made rural dean of the district; and in 1924 received the honorary title of Abbot-pastor of Porno.

The young administrator of Zalaegerszeg really administered! Homes, churches, convents, and schools were built; order grew out of chaos; and the people of the district learned they had both friend and father in the priest who spread charity everywhere, living its very spirit. The thin little children of the poor came to his house every day for the quota of milk he carefully provided out of his own substance. What he had, belonged to the poor. Stern with himself, he was also stern with his people, tolerating no shiftlessness or moral irregularities; making it his business to know the problems and difficulties of hundreds of families. His priests, like his people, both loved and feared him. Though frail, he drove himself without mercy, supervising church and social work in all of Zala County.

His poor country, now trying to establish a stable government following the Peace Treaty of Trianon which had shorn it of two-thirds of its territory–impoverished by war and revolution–had muddled through; and swinging again toward monarchy, was functioning in the name of the "Holy Crown of Hungary," having elected as regent Nicholas Horthy. King Charles IV remained exiled in Switzerland. Hungary was divided between those monarchists who wanted the return of Charles, and those who did not wish to discuss the question of the throne. Father Joseph, with the legitimists, was for Charles; and upon his death, for his son, Archduke Otto.

And now nearby there began the rise of a movement which would attempt to devour his country. Hitler had risen to power in Germany; and early in 1930 the Arrow-Cross party, masquerading as a patriotic movement to revise the Peace Treaty, but actually formed to spread the Nazi idea, had been organized in Hungary. It gained headway quietly, and it was not until 1935 that Father Joseph realized it was disseminating the doctrines of Nazism with all its anti-Semitism and anti-Christianity. Then again the warrior who had combatted the Communists in 1919 went into action. He called a general assembly of the county, and verbally tore the Nazi doctrines of the Arrow-Cross party to shreds, thereby calling down upon his own head a barrage of defamatory propaganda. Fearlessly, he continued to excoriate their leaders, and to support, as far as he could, those who opposed them and whose position was based on Christian principles.

The story about Father Joseph's change of name at this time, I'm sure you will find as delightful as I do, Saint Ignatius. The Nazi protagonists had gone so far as to suggest that all Hungarians of German descent (of whom Father Joseph was one) should drop their Hungarian names, and assume German ones. Father Joseph's people had always retained their German name, Pehm, through three hundred years on Hungarian soil; but the idea that those without a German name should adopt one was too much for Father Joseph. He signified his scorn by immediately dropping his *German* name, and taking the Hungarian name of his birthplace. From now on, he would be known as Mindszenty! He also seized every occasion to denounce anti-Semitism, calling it "the basest tool of Nazi propaganda—a tool which seeks to undermine the very foundations of Christian civilization."

Those in high places also defending the principles of Christ recognized his worth; Bishop Mikes appointed him Bishop's Commissioner in 1927, with authority to found new parishes; and the Holy Father himself ten years later conferred upon him the title of papal prelate.

But the Arrow-Cross continued its activity and Hitler his plans; and the second World War broke in fury on September 3, 1939. Hungary, although it had signed the Axis pact, proclaimed its neutrality—which meant less than nothing to Hitler. The heroic Paul Teleki, then Hungarian Prime Minister, refused Germany egress across Hungarian soil for the attack on Poland; but two years later when Hitler was ready to take over Yugoslavia, Teleki knew he couldn't win, and shot himself, rather than betray the nation with which his country had signed a friendly pact. In April, 1941, the German army entered Hungary, carrying into Yugoslavia torture and death to the Jews.

Mindszenty pleaded for mercy for the victims, and even sent messages directly to Hitler; but to no avail. Then one dark night in March, 1944, Hitler's armored columns marched into Hungary to occupy it. It was significant that only a few days later, a letter arrived at Father Joseph's residence, bearing the Holy Father's designation of Mindszenty as Bishop of Veszprem. So it was, dear Saint Ignatius, that he came to follow in that long Apostolic succession in which you were one of the first. As you had received it in the first century, now he in the twentieth was endowed with the authority to spearhead the battle for Christ. It was to rage fast and furiously across Hungarian soil. And perhaps it was at this time too, that Mindszenty began to have his own dreams and hopes of martyrdom.

As Bishop of Veszprem, new power had been put into his hands. He exercised it for the improvement of conditions in the concentration camps, the release of prisoners, and in helping the hapless Jews. Minor Hungarian officials now doing the will of the Nazis were yet Catholics; many dared not disobey their Bishop. It would seem that only the Christ you both loved kept Mindszenty alive at that time, so arduous were his duties, so multiplied the cries for help, so dangerous the risks he took. As the French would say: "*L'audace, toujours l'audace!*" His very daring seemed to confer on him a charmed life. But his poor country was now to see another invasion: that of the Russians from the east, marching to defeat Hitler. In great confusion the German surrender was signed in October, 1944; but not before the Nazis, knowing the war was lost, had wrought innumerable brutalities upon the Hungarian people.

Greatly concerned for those Jews who had not yet been "liquidated," the Bishop of Veszprem commissioned Bela Varga, a leader of the Small-Holders' party which had bitterly fought the Nazis, and who had been in hiding under Mindszenty's protection—to save the Jews in Budapest, utilizing every one of the Catholic institutions in the city as a secret refuge. Thousands of Jews were thus saved, while Mindszenty himself remained under the constant surveillance of the Nazis. Once he managed to elude them for a visit to the Jesuit monastery in Budapest which was Varga's secret headquarters. He had come to thank him for his great work. Both knew that upon Mindszenty's return to Veszprem, there was every probability that he would be taken by the Nazis; and Varga urged the Bishop to remain in hiding at the monastery. Then spoke the true martyr, the true "witness":

"Rome can find another Bishop if I die, but it will be hard to find followers, if today we run away from danger. *Believers are born through martyrdom!*" That was exactly as you had thought yourself in the first century, Saint Ignatius. So the Bishop started boldly back for Veszprem. To his disappointment, he was not arrested then; he became the more audacious and went straight to the Nazis to request that in their retreat from the Russians, they leave off making a battleground of eastern Hungary. It didn't take long after that. For the Nazis in Veszprem knew that he was sheltering twenty-six Jews in the basement of his residence; although in his efforts to hide them, he had permitted no one but himself to carry food to them. He was arrested on October 31, 1944. That was the famous time when he dressed himself in his full episcopal regalia, refused to be taken off quietly in a car, and collecting twenty-seven of his priests, insisted on walking to the jail at the head of the procession. Again by sheer force of audacity, he had won a point—for the people of Veszprem had a good view of their beloved Bishop being marched off to prison by the Nazis, as they knelt along the streets to receive his blessing. Later, another arrest was, alas, to be different....

Mindszenty and his staff were soon transferred to the penitentiary at Sopron, where again he appeared to woo martyrdom. Offered release upon condition that he sign a declaration of loyalty to the Nazis, he refused. Later he was visited by friends who urged him to let them arrange an escape. He answered that the only thing he desired to escape was possible deportation. "I wish to stay in Hungary, near my people," he said.

You might have thought, Saint Ignatius, that with the appointment of an Allied Control Commission which included the United States, things would have brightened; but you see at that time the Russians were our dear friends—it's very confusing, I know—and so we let them do about everything they wanted to do. It ended up with a puppet government acting on orders from Moscow; and their turning against us, just as in every other country they occupied.

First came the "land-reform," ostensibly to break up the large estates and give land to the peasants, but actually, as Mindszenty soon saw, a scheme to give each peasant so small a strip of land as to prevent his making a living from it, and so eventually to force the peasants into co-operative farms of the Russian order, working solely for the State. They threw the Bishop a sop, by exempting five hundred acres of episcopal land as a reward for his opposition to the Nazis; but this in no way stopped Mindszenty's outspoken opposition to the program. Later, what a weapon this proved to be, in the hands of his persecutors!

In the very month the Bishop was "liberated" by the Reds from his Nazi prison, the most powerful churchman in Hungary died—he who held the ancient title of Prince Primate, which carried authority in both Church and civil matters—Justin Cardinal Serédi. There was much ado, Saint Ignatius, about who should succeed him; and the government sent their own recommendations to Rome. They did not include Mindszenty. But the Holy Father saw matters differently. Early in October the official message was brought from Rome that the peasant-priest of Cseh-Mindszent had been designated Archbishop of Esztergom and Prince Primate of Hungary.

It seems significant, Saint Ignatius, that when he received the news he was standing before the altar in the great church at Papa, there to confirm some eight hundred children—and that he turned and pointed to the altarpiece, a representation of the stoning of the First Martyr, Saint Stephen. While he only spoke of love and tolerance, I have often wondered what his inward, private vision was at that moment; and later, too, when he finally got to Rome to receive, on February 18, 1946, the red hat from the hands of Pope Pius XII, after the government had hesitated to issue a passport (only granted through the intervention of the American Military Mission which flew him to Italy on an American plane). I wonder what his thoughts must have been when the Holy Father said: "Receive . . . this red hat, the sign of the unequaled dignity of the Cardinalate, by which it is declared that thou shouldst show thyself intrepid even to death, by the shedding of thy blood for the exaltation of the blessed faith."

It is said that the Pope then touched Mindszenty's arm, saying: "You may be the first whose red blood will stain the blood-red of the Cardinal's hat."

The peasant-priest, who was now Prince Primate, returned to Hungary and took up, simply, his residence in the bomb-ruined grandeur of the Prince Primate's palace in Esztergom—there to lead a life of utmost austerity. Since others suffered from the cold, he would not permit the palace ever to be heated. His diet was meager, he fasted much and gave everything he could lay his hands on to the poor. But almost at once the fur began to fly between him and the Communist authorities. Both the Protestant Church and the Catholic Church were united in their determination to fight the stranglehold of atheistic Russia upon their Christian land—and both looked to Mindszenty for leadership.

The Cardinal's first Pastoral Letter made clear the definition of Christian democracy, and stated boldly that in Hungary "it would appear that one totalitarian dictatorship is being relieved by another." He pointed to the attacks upon marriage; the confiscation of private and church property without compensation; summary arrests of innocent persons; imprisonment of priests; the denial of God—and urged his people to go forth to the coming elections and vote for a government which would respect "the natural law and God's Commandments." The people responded and elected a good government; but it was helpless in the hands of the occupying Reds. Hungary became a "Republic" on February 1, 1946, with a Protestant minister, Zoltan Tildy, as President; but the fingers of Russia began to close on the country more tightly than ever.

It was early in 1946, when the relentless campaign of propaganda against the Cardinal began. They must set about destroying him in this manner, for he not only held the love and respect of the people, but also the support of all anti-Communist forces in the land. They probably told themselves it would take about three years to complete his destruction—and so it did.

Meantime the martyr ever pursued his destiny. Once in Budapest a small procession of cars bearing priests, among whom was the Cardinal, was stoned by a mob of Communists. Mindszenty immediately ordered his driver to stop. Stepping out and facing the crowd, he cried: "If you want to stone the Church, stone me! I am the Church!" The mob fled. But the strong web of propaganda was being spun daily, frequently under threats. Devoutly religious citizens were asked to read aloud at meetings denunciations of the Cardinal; and if they refused, were arrested on one pretext or another. Little children in school were told to sign papers condemning the Cardinal as a traitor. Those who would not were dismissed from school. It was not long before sixty per cent of the schools which had been operated by the Church and various other denominations were taken over by the government to teach the children the doctrines of Communism.

In fact, it was the Cardinal's forceful protests against nationalization of the schools and interference by the State with the religious education of children which played the strongest part in his eventual martyrdom. How often in connection with it, Saint Ignatius, have I thought of your own comment when you wrote to the Ephesians: "Do not err, my brethren; they who corrupt families shall not inherit the kingdom of God." In Mindszenty's famous Pastoral Letter of May 20, 1946, he wrote:

"The prerogative of parents to educate their children cannot be disputed by the State, since it is the parents who gave life to the child. . . . It is their right to demand that their children be educated according to their faith and their religious outlook. It is their right to withhold their children from schools where their religious convictions are not only disregarded, but even made the object of contempt and ridicule. . . . You Hungarian parents must . . . feel a violation of your fundamental rights if your children can no longer attend Catholic schools solely because a dictatorial State closes down our schools by a brutal edict, or renders their work impossible. . . . Watch and pray, for your rights are at stake. The souls of your children and your grandchildren are at stake—in short, our whole future. . . . Let us rise in the spirit of justice, peace, human dignity, and freedom—for the education of Catholic youth."

These and similar outcries from the Cardinal against related abuses, coupled with his wide popularity and prestige, determined the Moscow-controlled government to do away with Mindszenty. Two-thirds of the population were Catholics. They must no longer be permitted to be "reactionary." Their Cardinal was protesting against the very pillars of Communist strength—State-controlled schools, compulsory membership in the Communist party, the secret police, dissolution of Catholic societies, prohibition of religious processions, compulsory spying, unjustified arrests, torture and murder. The bill to nationalize the schools was passed by the Hungarian Parliament in June, 1948—and upon the Cardinal's order, the bells of all the Catholic churches in Hungary rang loud and long in mournful protest.

Realizing that it would be less embarrassing for them if the Cardinal would just go quietly away, the Communists offered him a safe exit from the country. But he who was cast in the mold of a martyr did not respond. "I remain here," he said firmly. He was completely realistic about the fate awaiting him. "In four months," he declared to friends, "I shall probably be waiting my turn in a hangman's cell. But I shall never change my policy."

There had been one splendid chance to escape, when after many delays a passport was finally issued permitting him to visit Canada for the Marian Congress in the summer of 1947, and when at the same time he also visited Cardinal Spellman in New York. In New York many admirers urged Mindszenty to remain, pointing out that his return to Hungary would probably mean his death. And I have an idea, Saint Ignatius, that the martyr brightened perceptibly at the thought. He said: "The shepherd's place is with his flock." He returned to Hungary. Then, too, there was that time when Hungarian friends begged him to leave the country on the same grounds.

He shook off their suggestions. "A dead Primate is a greater power than a living one," he remarked.

Not only in the Pastoral Letters did he denounce the Communist-controlled regime, but also in courageous letters to the Prime Ministers. In these he protested civil abuses, exercising an age-old hereditary right of the Prince Primate. But it was a right constantly denied by the Communists. For the sake of his country, Mindszenty clung to it tenaciously; as for the sake of his Church, he emphasized constantly the authority of the bishops—as indeed, Saint Ignatius, you had emphasized it so many centuries before.

By now it has become more than obvious that the Communist plan is to destroy the influence of the hierarchy in order to weaken the organization of the Church, to separate bishops from priests, and priests from people—on the ancient precept of "divide and conquer." It would seem from your own letters, Saint Ignatius, that this was a threat imposed on the Church in its infancy, when you were Bishop of Antioch. You were as alert to it as was Mindszenty. Isn't it remarkable how the basic pattern of persecution remains the same through the centuries in the hands of those who would destroy Christ? Only the surface is different.

Almost immediately upon his return from America, the net began to close more firmly about the Cardinal. For months he had known he was being watched. For months the government-controlled press and radio had blasted forth denunciations and accusations that he was a traitor.

Toward the end of 1947, in a Pastoral Letter to his flock, he had written: "Although we are filled with grave sorrow for your souls, we shall not continue to communicate with you by printed letters, as has been the familiar way in other countries and other times. We are compelled to descend into the catacombs and to speak to you as the Church did four hundred and fifty years ago, during the Turkish oppression." Indeed, Saint Ignatius, as it had done in your time! There was little difference. Then he continued: "*We do not however give up the struggle for freedom and the independence of the Church.*"

People who have met the Cardinal have spoken of his simple, kindly dignity—but his firm, and at times almost stern, mien—so it's delightful to find, Saint Ignatius, an underlying humor in at least one of his letters. Writing to warn against a government textbook which had been introduced into the schools and which denied God's part in Creation and pronounced man's descent from the ape, he commented: "We understand very well why there is anxiety in certain quarters to proclaim man's descent from the ape." That was hitting them!

The fall of 1948 saw the beginning of the end. Early one dark November morning, his priest-secretary, the Reverend Andrew Zakar, was seized as he was returning from saying Mass at a convent. When the news reached the Cardinal, he knew that he would be next. Nobody knows exactly what they did to poor Father Zakar, but all agree that the treatment included brutal physical torture and drugs. Those sinister drugs, spawns of the devil, were probably actedron and mescaline—one to stimulate and one to "de-personalize" the victim.

A story is told that Father Zakar, following a seige of torture, was escorted from the prison to the Cardinal's residence by guards who ordered him to show them the hiding place of the Cardinal's confidential papers. Old comrades who encountered Zakar in the corridors of the palace at that time, related that his personality was completely changed. He was smiling and babbling, and introducing his guards (who so recently had tortured him) as "these, my very good friends"! Amiably and openly he led them to the Cardinal's papers—as though he were doing the most natural thing in the world.

And all the time he conducted a conversation with the horrified observers, his former colleagues, that was at complete variance with the Zakar they had long known. Later, when the Cardinal was informed of his bizarre remarks, he commented: "Within a short time I, too, shall be talking in the same manner." He knew the methods of the secret police; he knew what actedron and mescaline could do to the most stalwart victims.

In fact, Saint Ignatius, he knew so well that he sat down at his desk and wrote a memorandum to the Hungarian bishops, to be delivered secretly to them upon his arrest. In it he stated that he had been falsely accused; that he "had not participated in any conspiracy," and that he would not confess to such—but that *if* they should hear of any such "confession," they should "consider this but a sign of human frailty and regard it as null and void."

The Communists did not keep him waiting long. They chose December 26th, the day after Christmas. His mother was visiting him. Not in the open daylight, as Rome had taken you, Saint Ignatius, did they take him—but in the dark, when no one would see; when everyone was at home. The Cardinal and his household had just been at prayer in the chapel; now he and his mother stood side by side facing the armed police. Barely time to send for his hat and coat, barely time to embrace his weeping mother. It is said, Saint Ignatius, that this holy peasant-mother who had looked after him since he was a little boy and had always mended his clothes, even after he had become Prince Primate, for long had known in her heart that this day would some time come. Yet she was not one of those who had urged his escape—in fact, quite to the contrary.

Someone has related that he turned to one of his priests and said: "If the living Cardinal cannot help his country and the world, perhaps the dead Cardinal can." That compulsion of the true martyr—he felt it even as you had felt it, Saint Ignatius, on that long-ago day when the soldiers of Trajan put you in chains and marched you off to the wild beasts. Today, they don't use wild beasts—for men, in their emulation of them, can do so much better.

It would have been so much pleasanter for the Cardinal if they had simply killed him outright. But that would have defeated their purpose. They had learned from a long line of martyrs, from you among the first, that a courageous death suffered for a cause they would destroy, serves only to strengthen that cause.

The stories of the torture to which the Cardinal was subjected preceding his so-called "trial" make the hardiest soul flinch. He is said to have been imprisoned in that infamous "chamber of horrors," number 60 Andrassy Street, the headquarters of the secret police. There his inquisitors undertook the task of securing the admission of his "treacherous activities against the people's democracy, conspiracy against the republic, and foreign currency abuses." Questioned for hours on end, the Cardinal refused to "break." "No!" he shouted in denial to literally thousands of questions, some of which were repeated hundreds of times. For more than three days and two nights, he resisted unflinchingly. But they were out to get a signed "confession" before the trial started, and must get it at all costs, except that of his life.

It is told that when he persisted in his denials, to further weaken him they brought before him the physical wrecks of some of his imprisoned associates—among them, Father Zakar. Their faces and bodies had been tortured almost beyond recognition.

At last when they had succeeded in breaking his body so that it could no longer stand, but not his will, they began the diabolical treatment of the drugs. Actedron and mescaline are said to have been used—the first to stimulate, the second to "de-personalize" the victim, to change his normal character so completely that he would become an entirely different person. Do you not think, Saint Ignatius, that this is murder in a more diabolical degree than ever was shown by any of the great killers of history?

When finally the poor Cardinal had held out for eighty-four hours, the longest record ever achieved in the terror-ridden rooms of 60 Andrassy Street, tragically he signed a "confession." Of course he hadn't the faintest idea what he was doing! But it gave the Communists something to release to the world: the admission of Joseph Cardinal Mindszenty, Prince Primate of Hungary, that he was a traitor. Here indeed was the document of which he had privately warned his bishops—that "sign of human frailty."

With this document, plus others of equally dubious character, they could now open the trial and show the world that, even with a "confession" of his guilt, the "traitor" would be given the benefit of a truly "democratic" judicial procedure. Aren't the Communists funny, Saint Ignatius? They lack all sense of humor, remaining completely blind to the uproarious farce presented to the free world by their "democratic" trials. Perhaps, rather than for the conversion of the Russians, we should first pray that they acquire a sense of humor; and *then* pray for their conversion—for Christianity is a religion of joy, and has no place in it for the humorless.

Forty days after his arrest, on February 3, 1949, this amazingly democratic trial began. It was so democratic that the public was admitted (after showing a personal pass and identification papers) and, in seating, each person was paired off with a plain-clothes man of the secret police. So democratic that the press, alleged to represent "the public opinion of sixteen nations," consisted, with two exceptions, of Communist sympathizers. The two exceptions did not understand the language and had to use translators carefully selected by the government. So democratic that visas had been refused to special correspondents the world over; the Foreign Office stating that "local representatives, familiar with the circumstances," would report the trial. (Three of them were so "familiar" that they still bore the scars of weeks in the dungeons of 60 Andrassy Street for writing wrong impressions of the people's democracy.) No radio commentators or news photographers had been allowed to enter Hungary. Government photographers took pictures of the trial and, if passed by the censor, released them to the press.

It was so democratic that Mindszenty's choice of a defense attorney was refused. A tried and true Communist from the days of Bela Kun, back in 1919, was appointed to defend him. So democratic that the public prosecutor in the case was one Julius Alapi, a renegade Catholic with an unsavory past. So democratic that the President of the Court, Vilmos Olti, was a former Nazi.

Democratic to a degree that the government witnesses came straight out of the dungeons of the secret police. So democratic that "Radio Budapest," broadcasting from the courtroom to report the trial to the people, was systematically interrupted whenever the Cardinal's testimony began to throw doubt upon the charges. So democratic indeed that the defense attorney in his final summing up agreed completely with the prosecutor's charges against his "client"! He went on to extol the "freedom" and "fairness" with which the trial had been conducted. So democratic that forged documents were introduced as evidence. So democratic that the man on trial appeared to the blindest as a broken shell, a totally changed personality—dazed, confused, automatically responding as though under the influence of a powerful hypnosis. In fine, so "democratic" that the free world shuddered. . . .

So it was, Saint Ignatius, that the Prince Primate of that ancient Catholic land, Cardinal Mindszenty, stood accused successfully by the "democratic" people's court of Hungary of having conspired to restore the monarchy, to return the Hapsburgs to the throne, of having plotted with Otto of Hapsburg toward this end; of having attempted to cause the United States to intervene by force; of having conspired with the American Minister to Hungary; of having dabbled illegally in foreign currency; of having opposed the "land reform" and plotting to deprive the peasants of their land; of opposing the nationalization of the schools; and of blocking agreement between Church and State.

Humorlessly, he was even accused of not having co-operated with the Nazis (the same Nazis who had only recently been forcibly put out by his accusers) and thus the Soviet court went indirectly on record as supporting Hitler's anti-Semitic policy, since it was mainly on that Nazi policy that Mindszenty had not "co-operated." Putting an extra flourish on the ridiculous was the court's attempt to establish that Mindszenty was of noble blood and therefore not sympathetic to the people. This, of a man whose parents and grandparents had for generations been tillers of the soil!

The great martyr had the right, by Hungarian law, to have the last word at his trial. Despite his drugged condition, he made a mighty effort, declaring he had never been an enemy of the people; that he had never wished to deprive the peasants of their land; that he had always desired peace between Church and State. But he was too far gone to fight the travesty of justice which had been enacted during the seven days of the trial. They had seen to *that* previously, in the forty days when he had been their guest at 60 Andrassy Street. . . .

The Prince Primate was sentenced to imprisonment for life. He is more valuable to them alive than dead. For no one must say that the Communists are barbarians. Besides, this way they can bargain with him, as they would with a coin.

The official photograph of the Cardinal taken during the trial and stupidly released by the Reds (for in addition to lacking humor, they are also stupid) horrified the world. In it was read plainly the violent usurpation of a soul—the sin beyond all sins. Is not this living death of this great martyr of our time harder to bear than physical death, Saint Ignatius?

It is said that up to the very last moment he refused opportunities to escape. He forced them to arrest him. He deliberately chose martyrdom for the principles of Christ in the twentieth century, as you had chosen it in the first century.

Only a few weeks before the arrest, knowing he would be called to martyrdom, to be a "witness," he had written to his priests:

"To be a *witness* for Christ's sake is, above all, the calling of priests. . . . Their *testimony* must not leave the slightest doubt. . . ."

Then, quoting Saint Paul:

"They must now know more than ever before that 'we are made a spectacle to the world, and to angels, and to men.' "

("Spectacle" was the word for it, as far as *you* were concerned, Saint Ignatius, on that far-off day when they climaxed the Roman games with the sight of you in the jaws of the wild beasts.)

In this, his last letter, he again uttered thoughts so akin to those you yourself expressed. He spoke of the people united with their priests; of the flock at one with its shepherd.

"If one is not with the Bishops, he is not with the Church," he declared. That letter might have been written by you.

So I know that when his martyrdom is finally consummated, and he is taken home, the Bishop of Antioch will be the first to greet the Archbishop of Esztergom. You will clasp his hand, and call him "Comrade"—but not in the sense that the Communists mean it.

V

To Saint Thomas,
Apostle and Missioner

concerning FATHER GERARD DONOVAN OF MARYKNOLL

Dear Saint Thomas:

This has been rather a one-sided correspondence between us, although no one could blame you for not replying to that letter I sent you long ago. It was rather on the personal side, delving as it did into aspects of your life which were actually none of my business. Under the circumstances, a second letter would seem in questionable taste, were it not for the fact that now I am writing you about another. Almost, Saint Thomas, I can hear your sigh of relief!

The truth is that since writing you last, I have met someone who reminds me so greatly of you that I can no longer resist telling you about him. No doubt by this time you know him intimately; but it is quite possible that, from humility, he has not told you much about his life here on earth. There was a quality about it which showed a certain spiritual kinship with you, and which has endeared him in a special way to his contemporaries here below. For he is of my own generation, Saint Thomas, and moreover an American. You will understand, I am sure, the reasons for this letter, especially when you recall my long devotion to you.

This will introduce Father Gerard Donovan of Maryknoll. His brief but brilliant career for Christ seems strikingly like yours because, both missioners although separated by nineteen hundred years, you both carried the Gospel far into the dim East, and there laid down your lives in heroic testimony to its truth; you, according to long-established tradition, in sultry India, and Father Donovan in the cold mountains of Manchuria.

Father Donovan was very young when he died—only thirty-three. Significantly, that was the age at which your Master died upon a cross for all mankind, thereby setting the great precedent which guided you and all His Apostles, and has guided all His martyrs ever since. We do not know, Saint Thomas, how many years you labored as a missioner before the pagans in the far land to which you had journeyed killed you—but I have an idea you were older when you died than Father Donovan, because tradition tells us that you covered great distances, making vast numbers of converts to Christ before giving that last, glorious "testimony." Apart from India, there is even the rumor that you traveled to this hemisphere centuries before the discovery of America, and brought to the Aztecs in Mexico the beauty of His Gospel—a legend perpetuated by Lew Wallace in that unforgettable story, *The Fair God.*

But what is certain is that of all the great company of His Apostles, Father Donovan must have felt especially drawn to you—for you are the only one reported to have ventured so far into the East. When he was still a boy, he had turned his eyes wistfully in that direction, keeping them unwaveringly upon China until at last, at the age of twenty-seven, he made China his own. He had been only twelve when he confided to his mother that he wished to be a missioner of Maryknoll. It is related that she met the news bravely, saying: "God is in China, quite as He is here, Jerry. If you go there, He will surely be with you as He is here."

As befits the mother of a misssioner-martyr, she was an

heroic mother; such a mother as you must have had yourself, Saint Thomas. I wish we knew more of yours, but alas it was all so long ago that we can only conjecture that she was probably of the Jewish race, since you were among the first whom the Master called there in Judea. And there is also that plaintive question you are reported to have asked your Lord, as recounted in the Acts of Thomas, when He appeared after His Resurrection, and instructed you to carry the Gospel into India: "And how can I, being *an Hebrew man*, go among the Indians to proclaim the truth?" you wonderingly asked. Then before you knew it, you were suddenly speaking the Indian dialects like a native. On the other hand, poor Father Donovan, as brilliant as he was, had to study very hard to learn enough Chinese to carry His message to the modern pagans of China.

The Gospels do not tell us, Saint Thomas, just when the Master called you to be one of the immortal Twelve; but we know that it must have been in the early part of His ministry, not long after He had chosen Peter and Andrew, James and John, Philip and Bartholomew—and dear Saint Matthew, the tax-collector who loved to give parties. "And He gave them power over unclean spirits, to cast them out, and to heal all manner of diseases, and all manner of infirmities."

But that part of the glorious ministry imposed upon you and the others on which the young American, Gerard Donovan, must have dwelt the longest, was that unequivocal behest:

"Going therefore, teach ye all nations; baptizing them in the name of the Father, and of the Son, and of the Holy Ghost. Teaching them to observe all things whatsoever I have commanded you: and behold I am with you all days, even to the consummation of the world."

What a thrilling command, Saint Thomas! And how the

young Gerard must have envied you as he thought upon it: that *you* had heard these eternal words from the very lips of the Master. No matter how long one lived, surely one could never have forgotten the tones of that Voice. It must have echoed like an exquisite harmony in your ears throughout all the long journeys, making easy those most difficult paths. Down through the centuries it has called to millions; and so it came to pass that the light-hearted young Gerard Donovan heard it too, nineteen hundred years later, calling him from the modern Pennsylvania mill town where he was born into the vast, terror-ridden mountains of Manchukuo.

He would have envied too, that confirmation spoken directly of the Twelve: "And these signs shall follow them. . . . In My Name, they shall cast out devils: they shall speak with new tongues. They shall take up serpents; and if they shall drink any deadly thing, it shall not hurt them: they shall lay their hands upon the sick, and they shall recover." That was the accolade placed upon the shoulders of the Twelve in the first century; and when Father Gerard thought upon it, he would have felt very humble and very unworthy. And yet with a dauntless will, he determined to follow in your footsteps as closely as he, a child of the twentieth century, could.

For the deeds of the Twelve in fulfilling that timeless behest had spread His word everywhere. Indeed it was because of them that His word had eventually been carried into the modern river town of McKeesport, a short distance from Pittsburgh, where it blossomed most beautifully in the soul of the little boy born Gerard Donovan on October 14 of the year 1904.

His father, Michael Donovan, a master mechanic, had been born in Ireland, in the lovely County Kerry. His mother, Mary McCahill, was also Irish. They had been among the great number of immigrants to come to our shores in the era when the American industrial age was just entering its majority. And like millions of others, they had seen from afar that "mighty woman with a torch" who stands at the gates of the harbor of New York—that "Mother of Exiles." Across the seas, they had heard her call:

> "Give me your tired, your poor,
> Your huddled masses yearning to breathe free,
> The wretched refuse of your teeming shore.
> Send these, the homeless, tempest-tossed, to me.
> I lift my lamp beside the golden door!"

Perhaps you know, Saint Thomas, of these lines graven on the pedestal of the Bartholdi statue, the gift of France to our country—for they were written by Emma Lazarus, poet of your own Hebrew race. Gerard Donovan's parents, being Irish, had also been drawn to the young country by what was to them an even more compelling appeal. For is not this a nation whose cornerstone was laid upon the primary basic truth of God, as man's Creator? Alas, that in recent years many have sought refuge on our shores who, unlike Father Gerard's parents, would ignore that truth and destroy the cornerstone of the home which has sheltered them.

When Gerard was born, the thirteenth child, neither Michael nor Mary considered the number unlucky, so happy were they to welcome the little boy who was to become the pet of the entire family—particularly of his older sister, Katie. And while they were not rich, they enjoyed life in that small frame house which teemed with children in the carefree era of the early nineteen hundreds, when a man did an honest day's work for an honest day's pay; when food was cheap; when there were no income taxes nor labor overlords; no movies, no radios, no television; when entertainment was centered in the home and quite probably around an upright piano, not infrequently draped with an atrocious silk scarf—above all, when there were practically no automobiles. It was an American era uncluttered and uncomplicated by the mechanical aids which have since atrophied our powers of self-education and self-amusement.

It seems to me that, looking back upon that now far-off day, people actually supported themselves and lived within their budgets, poor and rich; and that the poor in their industry and self-respect, did not look to government or indeed, to anyone but themselves, for support. What a lovely America, it was in those days! It was also an exciting one for the young Jerry, growing up close to the green Pennsylvania hills, close to the river and the humming mills of industrial Pittsburgh.

I suppose, Saint Thomas, that boys are very much the same, the world over; yet there are certain things about the genus "American boy" which are perhaps peculiar to his breed. (The word "peculiar" I use advisedly, having myself grown up with two of them.) If you ever should take time to observe, you would note that the breed is characterized by an accelerated ingenuity and enterprise, with emphasis on the unexpected. For instance, its pockets. When turned out they can reveal an assortment of articles of great catholicity and frequently repugnant to the sensitive nostrils of the female, ranging from fishhooks to live snakes; carpet tacks to dead goldfish; water pistols to birds' eggs, and sundry.

Its standards, too, may differ somewhat from those of the young male of other nationalities. A bloody nose, for instance, marks it among its fellows with a certain distinction; a prestige similar to that which in England customarily attaches to important adults named to the Order of the Garter. Indeed, such a juvenile American nose proclaims as eloquently to its contemporaries as does the jeweled star of the British order: "*Honi soit qui mal y pense.*" Furthermore, the breed marks as pariahs, telltales and sissies. Whatever may be said for the lives of its parents, it can be asserted that they are never dull during the breed's formative years.

Jerry Donovan was as thoroughly an American boy as ever breathed, possessing in a generous degree all the characteristics of the breed. Small in stature for his age, he had the enviable gift of being able to make even his teachers laugh, which often saved him and his boon companions, among whom he was extraordinarily popular, from many a disagreeable *crise* of the classroom. Of all the stories of his lively youth, I am particularly drawn to that one concerning his first day in Saint Peter's parochial school. (A good name that, Saint Thomas!) To his older sister's horror, when she led him to his teacher, he greeted her with a broad smile which revealed a gorgeous gold crown upon his front tooth—cunningly contrived by himself from a piece of gilt foil. From the start, the youngest Donovan had the gift of the merry heart. It never left him, even through the bleak years in Manchuria, and endeared him to all who crossed his path.

Religion and mirth formed the aura in which he moved. An older sister was a nun; later, two older brothers were to become priests. Happy-go-lucky Jerry was a bright pupil, a lad who approached his studies with the same zest with which he tackled sports. And his smile was of a contagion to defeat the most dour of his elders.

Do you not find it charming, Saint Thomas, that Our Lord so frequently calls the mirthful ones of earth to His special service? How often have we heard the amazed question: "*She* will enter the convent? Impossible; she's too full of fun!" Yet the convent is precisely the berth in which "she" so frequently lands. So with Jerry Donovan. Possibly only his mother was not surprised. She must have known how much he had been impressed by Joe, the brother who was sixteen years older than he, and who was now preparing to be a priest of the Catholic Foreign Mission Society, which we all know lovingly simply as "Maryknoll." It was August of 1917, and Jerry was all of twelve, when he set his eyes toward the East, and his heart on the life of a missioner.

He may have told you, Saint Thomas, of his five happy years at Maryknoll Preparatory College near Scranton, and how it had been called "The Venard" for a young French missioner who long before Maryknoll was founded had also followed the path marked out by you, and at the age of thirty-one, in far-away Indo-China had "witnessed" with his blood for Christ, in the year 1861. Jerry must have pondered much upon the young martyr, Theophane Venard, between the studies, in which he became adept, and labor on the surrounding farm; between the rides on old "Gunpowder," the farm horse, and the camping trips and general merriment the young Donovan created wherever he went. His brother Joe had been ordained in 1920 and sent as a missioner across the Pacific. From then on, Jerry's heart was drawn more than ever to "the Field Afar." The same year saw his brother Tom also begin the way of a Maryknoller.

Father Jerry was ordained a priest of Maryknoll, in 1928, following his years of study at the major seminary at Ossining-on-the-Hudson, and a final year of special studies at the Catholic University in Washington. One can imagine, Saint Thomas, the joy that was his after the long preparation, the long dream of the true missioner, when on the afternoon of that great day, he received from the superior general of Maryknoll his assignment to China. But now almost at once began the true way of suffering of the missioner. Has he told you, I wonder, how only a scant month before he was to take ship for China, he was stricken while serving as guest-preacher at the church of Saint Thomas Aquinas in Brooklyn, and how he was rushed to the hospital, suffering from acute peritonitis? He and others were convinced that his last hour had come. Then, almost miraculously, he was saved through the skill of a great surgeon. But his strength had been so depleted that he now faced long months of convalescence. With heroically concealed grief as he lay upon his sickbed, he saw the long day slip by which marked the sailing from California of the mission band to which he had been assigned. The true priest had learned long ago to say, and to mean, "Thy will be done."

It is related that he also accepted cheerfully the prolonged period of convalescence at his old school, "The Venard"; speaking of his disappointment to no one. When able to work again, he taught the boys Latin and mathematics; and how they loved his Irish jokes narrated solemnly in Latin! His method as a teacher was unique. It was "laugh and learn," in Father Donovan's classes. Soon he was acting as procurator of the school, supervising additional building; working outdoors with the boys, building tennis courts, deepening the swimming pool. So high were his spirits, so everlasting his sense of fun, that it is said that if it had not been for his frequent presence in the chapel and his devotion to prayer, one might have thought of him as just another student. And few guessed how yearningly the inner eyes remained set upon the East.

At last, in the spring of 1931, came the summons so long awaited. The assignments of the superior general listed: "To the mission of Fushun in Manchukuo, Father Gerard Donovan, now of Maryknoll College." The boys cheered as the list was read at dinner. But only your Master, Saint Thomas, knew the upsurging gratitude which then overflowed Father Jerry's heart. . . . At long last, he had been deemed worthy to follow in your footsteps, in the footsteps of the immortal Twelve. . . .

He would sail from Seattle in August, and it is happy to reflect that before leaving for the West Coast he could pay a visit to his home in McKeesport, to be there for his mother's sixty-ninth birthday, spending it with her and his devoted sister, Katie. It is said that on this farewell visit his mother repeated the statement she had made when he was twelve: "God is in China, too, Jerry. He will take care of you there, as He does here," she assured him.

The missioners' path touched Japan, and went on into Korea, where other Maryknoll Fathers were to remain; and I read with such interest, Saint Thomas, in the light of our current war in Korea, how Father Jerry's journey with his companion, Father Comber, led him over the Yalu River and at last into Manchukuo, where he was to begin the real life of an Apostle. The Yalu River! In my ignorance, I confess that it meant little to me until last summer, when reports began coming to us of the brave struggle of our forces in Korea. And now as I think upon Father Jerry's brief life, and all that has happened since, the very name of the Yalu brings an involuntary shudder, a sense of foreboding and tragedy.

But certainly, he could have felt nothing but joy when he crossed that sinister stream, and set foot upon the promised land of his apostolate. He was not quite twenty-seven years old; for fifteen years he had clung to the dream which at long last was within his grasp. The same sort of exuberance must have possessed you, Saint Thomas, when at last you touched the far shores of India, which at that time must have seemed even more remote from Palestine than in 1931 Manchukuo seemed from McKeesport. Remote in distance, and remote in custom. How Father Jerry's merriment must have bubbled over at the difference! One can imagine the twinkling eyes with which he surveyed the primitive and the oriental, while at the same time his fine intelligence acknowledged an ancient wisdom, and his deep charity caused the warm heart to go out spontaneously to these people, now his spiritual "children." On the side, Father Comber must have found infinite amusement in his companion's lively comments.

It is pleasant, too, to reflect that along much of the journey there were veteran Maryknoll missioners to welcome them; as they were there at Fushun, the pioneer Maryknoll station, where Father Jerry was to assist the resident missioners, and learn to speak Chinese. He must have reflected rather ruefully, Saint Thomas, that upon your arrival in India, it had been made so much easier. But after all, when the Master sent the Holy Ghost to the Twelve with the gift of tongues, there had been no printing presses to create dictionaries. Besides, you were His especially *chosen* Twelve, as Father Jerry would have told himself with deep humility, while drawing his brows together over the infinitely multiplied Chinese characters; twisting his tongue around the strange-sounding syllables. He would learn that Mandarin dialect, or know the reason why!

It cost him many months of labor, but in the meantime he was busy every minute of the day, assisting Father McCormack, the pastor of the station; learning the work of the mission and of the thriving city of Fushun where flourished the largest open-cut coal mine in the world. Just beyond Fushun and as far as the eye could reach, the vast plains stretched: sparsely populated and primitive plains where the tall sorghum flourished for miles on end, and which, as Father Considine has pointed out in his memorable book, *When the Sorghum was High*, at its height can conceal the movements of vast numbers of armed men—the tall sorghum which was to play such a sinister role in the final destiny of the young missioner from McKeesport.

It was only three months after his arrival in Fushun that Father Jerry, with Father Gilbert as companion, rode gaily out to meet those plains upon his first assignment—a three-day journey, partly by train, partly on muleback, to take over his duties as curate to Father Frank Bridge, his old schoolmate, now pastor of the mission at Hsing Ching, ninety miles away. It is absorbing to reflect, Saint Thomas, that it was just such a missionary journey as you yourself must have undertaken many times, across wilderness and wild plains and mountains. Nineteen hundred years had passed, but in Manchuria as Father Jerry was introduced to it, time had registered little change. His mode of travel, on muleback, was the same as yours—the small inns at which the missioners stopped overnight as primitive and possibly as unclean as those which sheltered the Apostles on their far excursions.

Significantly, on this first journey of the young missioner, the discordance which was to interrupt from time to time the great orchestral opus which was Father Jerry's life in China broke the harmony briefly. A threat of bandits caused a village police chief to urge upon the travelers an escort of soldiers. The threat was one of which the veteran missioners made light; missioners being appropriately as poor as churchmice; and bandits, some of them at least, holding a certain chivalrous respect for these odd white men who went about with apparently no other purpose in the world than that of aiding the poor and the sick.

But only a few weeks after Father Jerry's arrival at Hsing Ching, again the disharmony sounded. On Christmas Day, following a beautiful midnight Mass at the mission which some of the Christianized Chinese had walked forty miles to attend, there rode into town a great company of soldiers to present the townspeople with the oddest of Christmas gifts—the heads of two hundred bandits surprised in their preparations to attack the town! To Father Jerry at that moment, McKeesport must have seemed very far away indeed.

But to ease any homesickness he may have felt, he was with his boyhood companion, Father Bridge, and from him he learned at firsthand how to be a Maryknoll missioner. Struggling with the language every day, he watched Father Bridge ride forth in a temperature of forty degrees below zero, accompanied by a Chinese catechist, on many journeys to remote villages, journeys which lasted sometimes as long as a week. Frequently upon returning, the fearless Father Bridge would speak of this or that encounter with bandits, from which, with his usual luck, he had emerged unscathed. As a bandit-of-sorts himself, he took converts by the score; and when Easter came, there were forty Chinese baptized in the mission chapel! But only a few months later, Father Bridge who had never spared himself, fell ill, so ill that he had to be taken over the long road back to Fushun. So it befell, Saint Thomas, that Father Jerry, within ten months of his arrival in Manchukuo, had become the mission pastor of Hsing Ching.

How I should have loved to have seen his domain! Apparently the mission compound, on the outskirts of the town, comprised a chapel, a school, a home for the aged, a house for the pastor and his curate, and a convent for two lovely old Chinese nuns. It was the nuns who had made for Father Jerry the warm, native clothing of corduroy and fur essential in the frigid winters. He loved the old people who were his charges and to whom the town merchants contributed rice and sorghum, and wine on their great feasts of the New Year, the Spring Festival and the Autumn Festival. But the little, slant-eyed schoolboys were his special joy. He took great pains in equipping their playground with swings and seesaws; and had a wonderful time himself when he could join in their games. That merriment which was an integral part of his nature made him their favorite companion.

But just when everything was organized nicely and the new pastor was ready to begin his journeys into the hinterland, that peculiar discordance again broke sharply upon the winter air. It was 1932. Bandits were again on the march, driving the frightened people of outlying districts before them like a swarm of bees. In they flew to Hsing Ching, to the mission compound, crying "sanctuary!" Piteously they looked to Father Jerry for food and shelter and protection.

It is related that the pastor made a comic business of the bandit threat, at the same time tirelessly seeing to the welfare of the refugees. Even when bullets began to whistle through the town, he regarded it all as a great joke. Meanwhile, the fighting between soldiers and bandits, partially due to a confused political situation, surged throughout the neighboring countryside. As he waited for calm, he sowed the good seed among the people of Hsing Ching, baptizing many among the refugees.

But by the fall of 1933, the city had become such a focal point of danger that it was necessary to build an entrenchment around it. The Maryknoll compound stood on its brink. Bullets swept through and around it. As Father Jerry dodged them with a grin, a fusillade hit the mission bell and set it clanging distractedly. When a lad, he had dreamed of the excitement of a missioner's life. Well, this was it! With apostolic zeal he forged ahead; and now the baptisms numbered about a hundred a year. His cup of joy was full when from out of these emerged one real vocation to the priesthood.

Then, off in far Lin Kiang, the most remote and widest spread of all the Manchu mission stations, a great pastor fell ill. Father Geselbrecht had broken under the strain and hardship of eight long years in that wild primitive country where his unmitigating labors had borne plenteous fruit, and Father Jerry was sent to relieve him. How pleased he was at this mark of confidence can be guessed, Saint Thomas, from his letter to the Maryknoll Center: "I have the privilege of trying to fill Father Geselbrecht's shoes—or rather, his seven-league boots!" After a six hundred and fifty mile journey around and over mountains, he reached Lin Kiang, the lumber center, and once again, that sinister Yalu River which he did not realize was later to play its part in the history of his own native land.

From the station here, according to the pattern laid down by Father Geselbrecht, he began his missionary journeys in earnest, traveling with the catechist, Wang Yun Chang, a tall and grave Oriental who had embraced Christianity with all his heart. More frequently than ever now, did the disharmony sound as Father Jerry and Wang rode up and down the mountainsides. Frightened refugees passed them, crying "bandits!" But the two rode serenely on. Had not Father Geselbrecht assured them that no harm would come to a missioner? In the valleys, through the nodding sorghum, they glimpsed silent horsemen who let them pass unchallenged; and so would come unharmed to the village of their destination where the Christians eagerly awaited the promised visit of the "Shen-Fu." Confessions; a night's rest among friends; early Mass and the road again, as village after village received Father Jerry's benediction.

They even blazed the Gospel trail further than had the intrepid Father Geselbrecht, carrying it to far Meng-Kiang, although their good friends begged them to turn back, so rife were the mountains with bandits. Soldier escorts were urged upon them; but Father Jerry waved them away. It was now, Saint Thomas, as though his heart had begun to reach out for possible martyrdom.

There was one city particularly where he lingered, and longed to return—Huai-Jen, which he confided to Monsignor Lane, "gives me a heartache." Thirty years before, a French missioner had carried the Gospel to Huai-Jen; but there had been no resident priest there in eighteen years. Under difficulties, a few good people had clung to the Faith; but the soft red poppy had nodded its sensuous head, tempting many to trade in opium. Others, under stress of poverty had turned to banditry. To Father Jerry, Huai-Jen was his loved "lost" city. He longed to lay siege to it and capture it for the Master. He would return one day, he told himself; and indeed he did, but in a manner more dramatic than he ever dreamed....

It is fascinating to reflect, Saint Thomas, on this, the missioner's work in the twentieth century, and your own of the first century, and to wonder if there is much difference. The great cause was, is, and ever will be, the same. The Voice that had sent Father Jerry to far fields was the same which had sent you and the other Apostles out from Palestine. "Going therefore, teach ye all nations; baptizing them in the name of the Father, and of the Son, and of the Holy Ghost."

And as one thinks upon it, the methods of the missioner seem not to have changed. Hadn't the Maryknoll Fathers done exactly as the Apostles had done, when they established first the mission center of Fushun, in Manchuria? The Apostles' first endeavor had been to establish a "church" in a given locality. From such "churches," or centers, spread out like the sun's rays, the itinerant journeys into the surrounding country. The modern missioners in China travel as the Apostles traveled: on muleback and in pairs. Paul and Barnabas had journeyed together to Cyprus, just as Father Jerry and Wang Yun Chang had journeyed to Meng-Kiang. When the Apostles' converts gathered about them it was for the sacred "breaking of the bread." The mountain villages of Manchukuo waited eagerly for the visit of the "Shen-Fu" to celebrate Mass.

I have so often thought, Saint Thomas, of how you and the others would enter a city for the first time and begin your preaching in the market place. While the market place is perhaps not practicable for such purposes today (although London has its Hyde Park and New York its Columbus Circle) still Father Jerry approached your method as nearly as he could. There in Hsing Ching he invaded the town barbershop. Apparently as much a social center as ever was the market place, it was there that everyone went to while away the time and to exchange news. So while the Chinese barber was busy at his art in one corner, Father Jerry had very sensibly employed a wise convert-catechist to expound the doctrine of Christianity in another. One could hear a first-rate sermon in one's native tongue, while the barber was snipping at one's beard. It worked like a charm, and many a seeker found his way from Father Jerry's barbershop to the mission on the outskirts of the city.

As for that macabre disharmony which disturbed the melody of his missioner days, had not Saint Paul written that he too had been "in perils of robbers"? Later, Father Jerry was to share with him certain of those other dangers: "in perils in the city, in perils in the wilderness . . . in hunger and thirst . . . in cold and nakedness." And finally, with you and Paul, and those other first great missioners, for love of Christ the barbaric death-stroke from pagan hands.

It was an odd thing, Saint Thomas, that having ignored the threat of bandits on the far, unbeaten track to Meng-Kiang, he and Wang were on the last lap of their journey home to Lin Kiang and presumably in safe territory when the first bandit struck. On a lonely stretch of road they heard, high above them, the eerie cry of a lookout; and knew at once they were marked men. Unswervingly they rode on. At length a horseman approached. Roughly he flourished a gun, ordering them into a thickly wooded ravine. Father Jerry must have felt as though he had stepped right into the Arabian Nights as he surveyed the bandit-king surrounded by his forty thieves, the most savage looking Mongol characters he had yet seen. But happily this bandit-king was a sort of Robin Hood. Observing the missioners' clothes, he reprimanded the captor, released them and waved them on their way.

Yet for the first time a note of seriousness crept into Father Jerry's attitude toward these gentlemen of the road. He wrote home to McKeesport: "Why these fellows treat us so courteously is a mystery . . . it certainly makes our work of getting around a whole lot easier. Some day, I may meet a crowd who are not so kindly disposed. But I leave that in God's hands."

Did he perhaps have a premonition, Saint Thomas? Certainly there were facts for one to feed upon, for soon the state of the land became so lawless that the Prefect Apostolic, Monsignor Lane, telegraphed from Fushun to all the mission stations to abandon travel until conditions should improve. Four years of the arduous work of a missioner had not dimmed the sense of fun in the light heart of Father Jerry. "You should have seen," he responded to Monsignor Lane, "how happy my mule was when I showed him your telegram."

There was plenty to do in Lin Kiang: a center to build where the hungry poor could come for food and warmth; there were the aged to care for, and improvements in school and playground. And when there was a brief lull in the activities of marauding bands, certain villages to visit again; and on one occasion, a trip up the Yalu River itself to say the Catholic burial service over the body of a brave Chinese soldier who with a group of only nine had died gallantly while holding sixty bandits at bay.

But ever nearer to Lin Kiang sounded the disharmony. Although its tones struck only upon that "inner ear," it jarred the soul as did that first air-raid siren which rang out over London in 1939, when the city fathers, anxious to devise an alarm sufficiently compelling to stir the Londoner out of his customary indifference, had created a calculated series of blasts conforming to what is known in the musical world by its gradation of sound, as "the Devil's Interlude." It was that, all right, Saint Thomas. I remember how fast the Londoners ran. And how I ran faster. The soul was shaken to its base by that crescendo of utter terror. It wasn't the airplanes that frightened us. It was that diabolical cacophony. Somehow I keep thinking of it as akin to the discordance which had advanced and retreated, and advanced again upon the inner ears of the missioners in Manchukuo at the particular time Father Jerry was laboring there.

For came that day of February, 1935, when news was brought that Father Clarence Burns, he who was stationed at Tung Hua, ninety miles from Father Jerry, had been abducted by bandits. Somewhere, away off in the forbidding hills, he was their captive. Would the fathers ever see him again? The method of capture had been low and treacherous, in accord with the best bandit standards. They had sent a messenger to the mission, begging for a priest to answer a sick call in a remote village. Poor Father Burns had hastened to the "patient" —who turned out to be not a sick man but, lying in ambush, a band of the huskiest desperados ever glimpsed on land or sea! Wu, his faithful catechist, was taken with him.

Father Jerry was greatly disturbed by the tragedy. He ran hither and yon, desperately urging the authorities to greater efforts, pleading for spies to send into the mountains. Two of the spies barely escaped with their lives. The months dragged miserably by, with no information, no hope. One can imagine, Saint Thomas, how the prayers rose upward from the missioners, and from none with greater ardor than from Father Jerry. He knew that too often the fate of a bandit-captive in those lawless mountains was starvation and death.

When at long last, after nine months of incredible hardship, Father Burns and Wu crept weakly back to their station, Father Jerry's voice led the *Te Deums* which mounted heavenward. Indeed, Saint Thomas, prayer was the only explanation that the two were still alive. Marked for death by their captors, they had the good fortune to be placed in the custody of one who was secretly sympathetic, and who turned his back upon their escape.

Meantime, Father Jerry's heartstrings were becoming ever more deeply attached to the wide mission of Lin Kiang where he had made a notable record in filling those "seven-league boots" of Father Geselbrecht. But in the summer of 1937, the melody was to go into a different theme which opened on a note both sad and joyous: sad, that he was called away from this beloved field; and joyous that the pastor he had replaced was now well enough again to resume his duties. In August, Lin Kiang welcomed back Father Geselbrecht and waved an affectionate farewell to the happy missioner from McKeesport who had filled so many of their hours with solace and merriment. Monsignor Lane had need of Father Jerry in Fushun to help with the central administration, and to serve as pastor at Saint Patrick's parish in Hopei, just across the river, and only a scant three miles from the central mission. "Now," he wrote his family, "instead of piloting the most distant mission, I am at the nearest."

The river was the Hun, and his new parish embraced a colony of Koreans—a name of as sinister import just now to all

Americans as is that of the Yalu—names that were to spell out tragedy for one young American from McKeesport back in the fall of 1937. In a sense, Father Jerry was the heroic advance-patrol of one—a spiritual soldier whose record many a military soldier of 1951 would come to venerate. Only the other day I read in a newspaper, Saint Thomas, the statement of General MacArthur that "the number of United Nations troops it would take to hold the parallel, would be sufficient to drive the Chinese Communists back across the Yalu River boundary with Manchuria, and to hold the line there." I hope that our boys who perhaps may again be fighting along those banks will not forget to ask Father Jerry's help—for I'm sure he will befriend them.

What a part those Manchurian rivers played in his destiny! He was to have crossed the Hun that afternoon of the fifth of October, 1937—crossed to Fushun, and the safety of the central station. But one thing after another delayed him as he bent hurried steps on the many duties demanding his attention in Hopei. Only a few short weeks had elapsed since taking over his new assignment. Finally he had sent Father Quirk across the river without him, promising to join him there later. Apart from the Koreans in Hopei, in whom Father Jerry was vastly interested, there were some five hundred Christian Chinese in his parish, and he was determined to give them of his best. To administer, there were the chapel and the rectory; the convent of the Maryknoll Sisters; a home for the aged; an orphanage; a catechumenate and a seminary. On that evening, he remembered that his new assistant, Father Rottner, just arrived from America, was to give Benediction in the chapel at six o'clock.

Hurriedly he finished the last chore before the bell should sound. Just as dusk was deepening it rang out over the chill October air. As he hastened to the chapel, those great mountains to the north whose foothills seemed almost to tread upon the streets of Hopei stretched bleak and mysterious into the unfathomable distance. The chapel was filling up with old men, old women, and children; for, as Father Considine has told us, the thick green sorghum was high and all the able-bodied men of the parish were busy at the harvest.

Having vested in the sacristy, he moved out into the sanctuary where he knelt in prayer waiting for the Benediction to begin. As he prayed, looking up into the eyes of the Crucified One, did he perhaps see, stretching immediately before him, his own Calvary? For it was about then, Saint Thomas, that the stranger entered the sacristy.

Young Francis Liu, a seminarian of seventeen, who was preparing the charcoal for the incense, looked up in surprise. Strangers did not enter here. But the rough-looking visitor brushed past him, and went on into the sanctuary itself, and stood there before the high altar. The congregation which had begun to chant the rosary, watched, puzzled, as he approached the kneeling Father Jerry. In a questioning, bewildered manner, he held out a paper. It was no place, Father Jerry decided, to answer questions; so he arose, and bowing the knee for the last time before the tabernacle where dwelt his Lord, escorted the stranger back into the sacristy. Meantime, the congregation continued to chant the rosary as they wondered what manner of urgent message was this—to call the "Shen-Fu" from the altar itself!

They could not see into the sacristy. They could not see the stranger whip out a gun, nor hear him threaten death to all in the chapel unless priest and youth would "come quietly." For Father Jerry, there was no choice. For almost immediately a second bandit entered. It became apparent that there were more, lurking outside. As priest and youth, unseen by the congregation, passed into the yard with a gun at their backs, an ancient handyman, Lao Kao, at work there, looked up in wonder. One of the strangers thrust a paper into his hands. "Give this to the foreign devils," he commanded, pushing his captives before him.

Beyond the gate, out of sight, three other sinister figures loomed. Quickly they bound the helpless two, and started them off at a quick pace toward the mountains. Two or three old men in the rear of the church, disturbed at their devotions by the rough voices outside, had emerged to investigate. In trembling horror they watched the strange procession of seven melt rapidly into the mountains. Their beloved "Shen-Fu" had been taken captive! They were old and feeble. They had no guns. Tears ran down their faces as they stood there, helpless.

And that was how, Saint Thomas, that Father Gerard Donovan of Maryknoll, Father Jerry of the light heart, went to his long martyrdom. Somehow it seemed as though it were something that his Lord and he had agreed upon long ago. Otherwise the police, a squad of twenty who went in pursuit but a scant half-hour later, might not have searched the hills in vain throughout the long dark night. Otherwise, the machinery of the American consulate at Mukden, immediately set to work, and the network of searchers spread out by the military commander might have been of some avail. The sorghum was indeed high, for the bandits and their prey had vanished as though the ground had opened and swallowed them. Frustration met all efforts. The American legation at Peiping was helpless. Even a company of reformed bandits who knew the mountain hide-outs searched without success.

Monsignor Lane, the missioners at Fushun and other places, the Sisters, the old people and the orphans grieved; while the hearts of certain ones in far-away McKeesport were desolate. The mysterious paper thrust upon the quaking old Lao Kao was, of course, a demand for ransom. Fifty thousand dollars in Manchu money, or about fifteen thousand in ours. . . .

It was the bandits' plan, following forced marches through eleven long nights, and after they were hidden at a safe distance, to send back the young seminarian to collect the ransom. Eventually the terrified Francis Liu appeared with their message. The missioners were overjoyed when they learned that he had left Father Jerry unharmed and in the hands of a bandit-chief known as Swang Shan, who was reputed to be less barbarous than others. They believed they could persuade Swang Shan to release him—not with ransom-money, for that would have opened the door to a consistent series of abductions, but by means of the reasonable plea that they had no money, and urging the captive's release on the grounds of the great good he and his fellows had wrought for the people. The letter was signed by Monsignor Lane, and written in Chinese and in English. Four men comprised the company sent by the government with the missive. Only one returned. And the missive was never answered.

Then came the news that seven of the bandits had been killed by soldiers; and that upon one of the seven the English letter had been found. No one ever knew whether the dead man was Swang Shan himself or a lieutenant. Quick on the heels of this information followed the report that the American hostage had been taken over by a much larger company of bandits, commanded by a man notorious for his cruelty. Again, no one ever knew whether Swang Shan had been defeated by the larger group, or whether he had cold-bloodedly sold his captive to them. But now indeed did the hopes of his friends sink to their lowest ebb. Perhaps it would not be, after all, as they had hoped—as it had been with Father Burns—that somehow an escape would be effected. The prayers and the novenas went upward with renewed fervor. The winter had come on in all its bitterness. How would Father Jerry fare in the mountain fastnesses with no warm clothing? Perhaps with no food? They redoubled their efforts and their prayers.

It was February of 1938 when they finally learned. Father Jerry's body had been found on a mountain path near far-away Huai-Jen—that loved "lost" city he had longed to save. In some mystical way, perhaps he has, Saint Thomas, for many now consider that a saint died upon its threshold. Curiously, it was a Chinese Communist bandit, a captive of the army, who revealed the tragic news.

When they went to claim him on February 10, they found the indelible marks of a long suffering. His body was thin and haggard; two toes had been frozen before death. There was a bruise over his right temple—and about his poor thin neck the rope that had strangled him. He had lain for perhaps a fortnight there, in the cold and in the snows. He had become a burden to his captors. So they had crushed his throat and left him there. For Father Jerry, the discordance had at last ended. And the heavens rang with a glorious melody which only he could hear.

And although his end, after laboring there in the East for his Lord, was different from yours, Saint Thomas, I feel you would be the first to welcome him into the great company of martyrs. Had he not been eloquently "testifying" to Christ, on his knees there before the tabernacle of the Hopei chapel when they came to take him? Had he not gone willingly, to save his flock from violence and death? Francis Liu had related how courageously Father Jerry had borne the abduction; how cheerful he had remained; and how he had comforted the frightened, weeping Francis. The youth had recounted how, true to the sunny heart within him, he had even amused his captors. Above all, how from the start he had utterly discouraged their attempts at ransom. A lesser soul would assuredly have sent back a plea for payment of the ransom, which would have meant freedom and life.

As the modern missioner to the East had faced death there in those cold Manchukuo mountains, I feel so certain that he must have thought of you, Saint Thomas, the first missioner to the East, and asked your help at the end. In the long months of captivity, he had ample time to reflect upon the courage of the first Twelve who had gone forth at the Master's bidding, baptizing in the name of the Father, and of the Son, and of the Holy Ghost. Thinking upon that great story, he would have drawn fresh courage to meet each dreadful day with its cold and hunger, its alarms and brutalities, its utter hopelessness. He had baptized many in China; had become beloved by the poor, the aged, the orphans and the sick; but his captors he could not baptize, because of "the hardness of their hearts."

Reviewing his own life, starting with his vocation and reflecting upon the journey he had made up the steep, spiritual path—the discipline, the learning utterly to forget self, to bear disappointment with a smile, to have no will but that of the Father—he would have thought of your own journey along the same path, nineteen hundred years before.

With sympathy, he would have reviewed your first steps, when close upon the Resurrection, the Apostles had cried to you: "We have seen the Lord!" He would have understood the impetuosity of the reply, partly a cloak to conceal the disappointment you felt at missing so great an event:

"Except I shall see in His hands the print of the nails, and put my finger into the place of the nails, and put my hand into His side, I will not believe!"

Father Jerry knew that as soon as you had uttered those words, they had begun to trouble your heart. For eight long days you had carried about that unhappy feeling, until at last our Lord showed his special love for you, by returning. It was both to comfort and to chide. In your unhappiness, almost you had prayed for the chiding.

"Jesus cometh, the doors being shut, and stood in the midst, and said: 'Peace be to you.'" And then, to you: "Put in thy finger hither, and see My hands; and bring hither thy hand and put it into My side; and be not faithless but believing."

With Father Jerry, I have loved, Saint Thomas, the spontaneity and fervor of your cry: "My Lord and my God!" And as he must have reflected, so often have I upon the event which followed, and which showed that there were others, too, in that great company, in whom faith must be confirmed:

"At length He appeared to the eleven as they were at table; and He upbraided them with their incredulity . . . because they did not believe them who had seen Him after He was risen again."

In this manner, through first learning the great lesson of faith, had you started climbing the steep grade to Heaven. Father Jerry must have thought too, of how the path had widened for you when at the Master's behest you had set off to carry the Gospel to far India. A builder of sorts himself (there had been that time at The Venard when he had supervised new construction, built tennis courts, and later in Lin Kiang when he had built a shelter for the hungry poor), he would have pondered upon your own building activities, which in a sense led to your martyrdom.

The story is a lovely one, Saint Thomas. I can see that mighty king of India, Gundaphoros, searching far and wide for a master-architect who would build a fairer palace than had yet been seen in the land. Like many a prince, he eschewed local talent and desired a foreign craftsman. The legend goes that his agents literally "imported" you, "an Hebrew man," as you called yourself. It must have been, Saint Thomas, that you were already a builder of note.

The manner you took of converting the king surely was rather startling to him. Returning from a long absence during which you were supposed to have completed the palace, he found not a stone laid, and all the money he had left with you for its construction spent upon the poor. One could not blame him, Saint Thomas, for being somewhat disturbed. It is related that you were about to be flayed alive when suddenly the king's brother, Prince Gad, died. After a glimpse of Paradise, almost immediately he returned to earth, to tell his brother of the beautiful palace he had seen there, marked as the property of the king and erected by your wise dispersal of his funds. Gundaphoros at once released you from prison, became a Christian, and gave all his goods to the poor!

But unhappily, so the story continues, another Indian king of a different caliber eventually crossed your path. King Mesdeus, thoroughly disapproving of the total conversion of his entire household, determined you were a sorcerer and ordered your death. It is related that he had you taken to a distant mountain where the people whose hearts you had won could not witness the crime—and that there you were speared to death, proclaiming Christ unto the end.

Father Jerry would have reflected that only the lonely mountains and a handful of "mercenaries" had witnessed your martyrdom. Only the lonely mountains and a handful of bandits were to witness his own murder, as he probably foresaw while the cold grew daily more intense, and his poor frozen feet were no longer able to keep up the fast pace of the bandit trail. He would have thought upon the ancient shrine of your martyrdom there on Mount Saint Thomas, near Madras, but never have dreamed that perhaps one day a shrine of his own might come to mark that mountain near his loved lost city of Huai-Jen, where they took his life.

And although he was too humble to have foreseen it, I feel sure, Saint Thomas, that over there in Manchukuo there remain many of his yellow friends whom he led to Christ, and who might well call themselves the "Father Jerry Christians" —even as today there exist, in southern India, a large number of persons who proudly call themselves the "Thomas Christians," descendants of those you converted almost two thousand years ago!

It is related of Father Jerry that he loved to sing, and it would seem almost certain that at times during his long captivity he had raised his voice to cheer himself and his captors, just as you had raised yours in the prison of Gundaphoros in that beautiful "Hymn of the Soul," your own composition, known as "the great gem of Syriac literature."

Because this modern missioner to the East had trod as closely as he could in the footsteps of the first missioner to the East, I feel sure that at the end you stood by him there in Manchukuo, Saint Thomas, and assured him that his "testimony" for the Master you both served would be recorded in the golden book of missioner-martyrs. For as though the words had been uttered but yesterday, he had obeyed to his utmost that behest: ". . . baptizing them in the name of the Father, and of the Son, and of the Holy Ghost. Teaching them to observe all things whatsoever I have commanded you." To his own particular martyrdom, they had taken him literally from the feet of his Lord—he who in his constant disregard of bandits throughout all the early perilous journeys had seemed in truth to court martyrdom.

And when the light-hearted American at length looked into the eyes of death, I'm wondering if the Master Himself did not whisper to him—to this one who in a sense had never grown far from the boy who on his first school day had gaily displayed a gold tooth of gilt-foil—did not open His arms and whisper to him the promise He had made His first missioners: "For behold, I am with you all days, even to the consummation of the world."

VI

To Father Pro, Martyr of Mexico

concerning **SAINT LAWRENCE**

Dear Father Pro:

Of all the martyrs to whom I've written, I approach you with the least trepidation—patriot, player, poet, and martyr of Mexico! For, being an actor, you should be the least startled. It is in the nature of actors to receive fan letters from ladies, so this missive should not make you turn a hair. True, when on this earth, you differed from the usual actor in many magnificent ways, because foremost, you were a player set apart by God for His special service. As such you had neither egotism nor vanity, two not uncommon qualities which enable actors to face fan letters with equanimity, nay, it is said, even with pleasure. So I cannot actually hope you will be glad to hear from me, but only that you will understand the compelling urge which prompts this indiscretion.

Let it be confessed at once that you have completely won me. That over, there are a thousand things I long to discuss with you. Of course I know you won't take me seriously. You took very little seriously when you were a part of our world, except matters which pertained to your Lord and the great task He had set you here on earth. For the rest, I'm afraid, Father Pro, that everything seemed a gigantic joke to you—including yourself. It is claimed that persons who cannot laugh at themselves have no real humor. But real humor bubbled from you in a perpetual fountain of eternal youth; and in those charming letters which careful biographers have collected we find you constantly poking fun at yourself.

For instance, when as a hunted Jesuit you were doing that superb piece of acting—portraying a gay young student as you moved about Mexico City, but actually bent on the important business of saving souls—apparently you reported to one of your superiors:

"I go about . . . sometimes on my brother's bicycle. I owe him already a fine bruise on my left arm and a lump on my head. . . . Very elegant, on my brother's bike, off I go, the bit between my teeth, through these streets of God, at the risk of my life. For the truck drivers here are most brazen! . . . In the outlying quarters, I talked, I shouted, I *bleated*, before my shirtless audience."

But even before you were called upon to play this dangerous role, it is related that when at the clinic in Hyères on the French Riviera trying to recover from three ghastly operations, upon visiting others who were patients, you would finish off a beautiful spiritual discourse with a broad wink and the question: "Now, *aren't* I the saint!" And all the time you were concealing your own terrible physical pain.

Later, you were to write of the persecution in Mexico:

"The first to suffer will be those who have put their hand into the religious question. . . . God grant that I may be among the first! If that happens, mind you all get ready with your petitions for when I'm in Heaven."

Indeed, it would seem that you were constantly kidding yourself, Father Pro—and let us admit at once, others. For example, those dear, pious old women for whom you conducted a spiritual retreat, and of whom you wrote: "I began with an audience of about ninety old ladies. Their ejaculations, sighs, sobs, and groans showed me something very clearly; and that was, if I was able to play upon the chords of sentiment, I myself had considerable difficulty, on seeing their lacrimose faces and spasms of woe, in repressing the laughter of my natural man." Could it have been, Father Pro, that the laughter of your "natural man" was somewhat in excess of what is natural to most men? In any case, it appears that you suffered from no shortage.

As for those old girls, being a woman, naturally I'm going to stick up for them when I read that you further wrote: "I judged it wiser to cut loose from the feminine gender, and go over to the masculine." For shame, Father Pro! Perhaps they did sigh, sob, and groan, and get their poor old noses all red. But that could only show the truly religious feeling natural to all women. Let me ask you if the red noses were not to be preferred to the behavior of certain men in church, who turn a "dead-pan" face to the preacher, and make off, hotfoot to the golf links before the last prayers are said?

Not only were those pious old ladies the victims of your sense of fun, but when I think of how you kidded the dignified minions of the law, set upon your arrest in Mexico City, I become almost sorry for them. How would you like it, if you were a policeman all dressed up in the sort of uniform popular in Mexico, with fancy buttons and feathered hat suitable to your station, and discovered that the debonair young student with the jaunty cap whom not two minutes before you had obliged with a match was, in truth, the notorious fugitive Jesuit whom it was your job to capture? When the poor bewildered policemen ran after you and turned a corner, lo, there was no student in sight. To be sure, there was a hatless cavalier escorting his lady by the arm, and leaning over her in ardent attention. How could they see the cap concealed under your coat? Or know that on rounding the corner you had fortuitously encountered one of your penitents who also had a quick gift for acting? Imagine how foolish they must have felt, and how hot and breathless, after they had run up and down several blocks, and found you had evaded them again! You did give them rather a hard time of it, Father Pro —what is worse, I'm afraid you enjoyed every minute.

There were also, when you were a boy, your poor teachers. Like all great actors, you had the gift of mimicry, and such mobile features as to permit the assumption of the facial expression of any type you cared to choose. It is related that you could even express a characterization with one side of your face; and, at the same moment, another with the opposite side. Thus, in school, when called to the teacher's desk, you could present a profile to the class which sent them into what is commonly known as stitches—while simultaneously presenting to the teacher the appearance of a veritable Job. All I can say is, I'm glad I wasn't one of your teachers. Until you grew up, they led a hard life.

Although perhaps not theologically correct, I can't help but believe that there is laughter in the heavenly courts, Father Pro. Nor can I help thinking what a good time you must be having up there, nor resist speculating on your companions. By this time you have learned, of course, how to appreciate women; and so you must surely be a friend of the great Saint Teresa whose Spanish blood you shared, and whose sense of humor is famous. You must surely also be drawn to my own countryman, Father Donovan of Maryknoll, who laughed his way through bandit-ridden China not many years after you had laughed yours through persecuted Mexico.

Among the ancients, of course you find particularly congenial Saint Basil the Great. According to Agnes Repplier, when summoned before the pagan governor who threatened that if he persisted in his Christian "error," he would have his liver torn out, Basil replied: "Do! As located, it has never given me anything but trouble."

But above all a martyr among martyrs, I think you must feel the greatest kinship with Saint Lawrence who, according to an age-old tradition, jested with his executioners as they were roasting him alive on a gridiron. "Turn me over now. I'm quite well done on this side," said he. It was actually a gigantic jest which landed him in this uncomfortable position, a jest which he could not resist playing upon the grasping prefect of Rome. As an archdeacon and custodian of the goods of the Church, he was ordered to produce its treasure. The Emperor thought it would make a nice tidy bit for himself. With the same sort of humor you yourself would have shown, Saint Lawrence assured the prefect gravely that, if given twenty-four hours to collect it, he would present the treasure. Rubbing his hands in anticipation, the prefect granted the extra day. At the appointed hour, Saint Lawrence led him into a huge chamber. There, in place of chests of gold and silver, rich ornaments and jewels, the startled prefect beheld an assemblage of all the poor of Rome—the aged and starving, the crippled, the lepers, the ragged widows and the orphans. "This," said Saint Lawrence, "is the treasure of the Church!" And one can almost see him, Father Pro, standing there, laughing at the enraged prefect. When the prefect looked about for the money and the golden vessels of the Church, there weren't any. Lawrence had spent a very busy day distributing it all among the poor. He was a charming youth. But neither of you seemed to have a proper respect at all for the duly constituted authorities. His flaunting of these brought about his martyrdom, as surely as your own was brought about by making those serious Mexican policemen the butt of all your jokes. (I can hear you both say: "It was worth it!")

In any case, it is lovely to reflect that you have found him there in Heaven, as congenial and understanding a friend as though he had died with you in 1927, instead of long ago in the year 258. The essence of humor was the same then as it is today; and the essence of martyrdom identical. After all, the divine gift of humor, and the priceless glory of martyrdom, both stem from One Who is Changeless. Nor are they restricted to any single nation. Of your humorous companions in Heaven, Saint Teresa is Spanish; Father Donovan is an American; Saint Basil comes from Asia Minor; Saint Lawrence is claimed by Spain; and you were born in Mexico. I need not remind you that the day was the thirteenth of January, 1891.

Your youth seems to have had a great deal of charm about it. How pleasant it all must have been, Father Pro, growing up there in the mining city of El Saltillo, the capital of the important State of Coahuila. Señor Miguel Pro, the handsome mine-owner and operator, and your mother, Señora Josefa, had created an ideal home for their growing family, with plenty of servants and comforts and, above all, religion. There was an older sister, and two younger, and there were three younger brothers with whom to play. With you in it, it is impossible to contemplate the Pro nursery as anything but a lively spot. It seems almost certain that you must have begun your dramatic performances right there, to the huge delight of your brothers and sisters; and I would give anything to know if you weren't on occasion surprised in the act of versatile impersonations of your elders. It is recounted that at this age, you had developed a fine taste in *tortillas*, those delicious cakes of maize, and in sweets–indeed, so fine that you opened your own charge account with the sweetshop. When the sizeable bill was presented, your mother paid it; but not without exacting a certain payment from you, not exactly in kind, but of the rather painful nature best remembered by small boys.

Two things, particularly, speak to us of your childhood and youth: the devotion to family, and the love of Mexican soil which was bred in you from its very depths, as it were, when you began to work for your father in the mines. How you loved those mines, finding a fascinating thrill in descending deep underground, plumbing the mysteries of the very heart of Mother Earth! In those days, it would seem as though you had no other desire than to be a miner, for you had come to love the strong men at whose side you worked, their courage and skill. Here, too, was built that enduring devotion to the common man which you never lost. It must have been that at that impressionable age you listened to many a story of the workers' problems, and were probably a frequent visitor to their homes. Young though you were, they found in you a sympathetic friend who ardently wished to improve their state. Although destiny was to carry you far from the mines, all through your life you loved them. They called to you as the sea calls to a sailor; and in your later ministry which spread a benediction on all classes, the cause of the working man, the laborer, lay nearest your heart.

Yet what actually pointed out your destiny and changed your entire life, was not the mines, not the workers, but that strong devotion to family which only a youth reared by such a mother, a genius in creating a happy home, could have felt. The evenings, the holidays, had been so pleasant, there in the cool patio with the gay young brothers and those lovely sisters. Merriment and music, as you regaled them with your mimicries, strummed the guitar to their singing, and beat out the time on your castanets to their dancing.

How you must recall, as though it happened but yesterday, that day when you returned from the mines to be met with the cataclysmic news that two of the beloved sisters were to become nuns. Impossible! How dared they break up that wonderful home, put an end to all the good times by going off to bury themselves lugubriously in a convent? It was unthinkable. It wasn't like them, this imbecility. Some dastardly influence had been wrought, by an enemy. Ah, the Jesuits! That was it. They had been your sisters' spiritual directors. In great perturbation, you tried to convince the lovely, soft-eyed girls of their error—and when your pleading availed naught, out you flew from the house like a madman. You wouldn't return. No!

Dear Father Pro, one thinks with sympathy of the shocked, heartbroken youth who fled that day to the hills for comfort. Even your mother had stood against you. Were they all mad, you asked yourself. It must have been a terrible hurt, for it is related that you stayed three days and nights in the wilderness, not caring how you slept or whether you ate, until finally your poor mother, worried to death, came and found you.

One can imagine that she must have told herself that she, who knew her Miguel better than anyone, had never dreamed that he was capable of such intensity of devotion; that he could feel so deeply. It was a wonderful trait, she reflected, but one that needed guidance. She knew that far back, commingled with your Spanish blood, was the hot blood of the fierce, proud Aztecs which had responded to the gentle law of Christ brought them by the early Spanish Franciscans, Dominicans, and Augustinians, in the days of the *conquistadores*. She needed no psychiatrist to advise her. Since she had plumbed to the root of your unhappiness, the treachery of those Jesuits, she would urge you to seek out the Jesuits; in knowing them, your resentment would vanish. What we don't know, we fear and mistrust. It is obvious that only because you loved her so much, did you consent—and that was like you, Father Pro.

Yet the success of her stratagem surprised even the Señora Josefa, when at length you returned from making a long retreat with the Jesuits, and announced that you would become a Jesuit yourself. And that was how God called the ardent young hot-head of twenty, Miguel Pro, to His service—in circumstances as dramatic as any which marked his essentially dramatic life. The soul which could love so intensely had found the Source of all love, and was at peace.

Yet the smiling young man who on August 10, 1911, entered the Jesuit novitiate of El Llano in the State of Michoacan, gave, we are told, few exterior evidences of the deeply mystical life which had begun for him. Into the seminary he carried his music and his jokes, enlivening the scene for professors and students. With joy I recall that episode of the sermon, Father Pro, and hope you won't object to the reminder. For I can see, as though I had been there myself, the athletic field during that period of recreation when you grew bored with the long argument on rules which had interrupted the game, and suddenly made for one of the goal posts. Now you might say that you climbed it; but in American parlance you "shinnied up" it, and clinging with one hand while you gesticulated with the other, regaled the students with a splendid imitation of a good Jesuit sermon.

Imagine your surprise when the laughter suddenly stilled, and from your precarious perch you looked down into the grave eyes of the Master of Novices. When you started in confusion to "shinny down," he held up his hand. "Remain where you are," he said pleasantly. "And begin again at the beginning. I missed the first part." History does not relate whether your eloquence had lost some of its zest as you went through the sermon a second time for his benefit.

It is sad to reflect, Father Pro, that for all the happiness of those days at El Llano, contemporary history was throwing its dark, forbidding shadow aslant their sunshine, filling the hearts of masters and students with uncertainty and a sense of imminent misfortune. They realized all too well what had befallen Mexico since the year 1821, when Spain had lost her last hold upon the country. Revolution, bloodshed, had followed. A republic had been proclaimed in 1825; then in 1848 had come the loss of half of Mexico to the United States. The revolutionary, Juárez, had seized control in 1858 and inaugurated that persistent persecution of the Church which was to endure, off and on, up to and through your own time. To successive lawless leaders, the rich properties of the Church were a tempting bait.

Civil war had broken out when the conservative element attempted to restore the work of the Church, the orphanages and schools, the institutions which had civilized Mexico. Porfirio Diaz had brought unity during thirty-three years of beneficent rule, while the anti-religious "Laws of Reform" were ignored, and the Church went about its work in peace. Alas, that the ambitious Madero was able at length to oust Diaz, only himself to be overthrown by revolutionaries three years later, in 1913. With the capital itself a battlefield, certainly it was not an auspicious year to take your first vows as a Jesuit. Had Huerta, elected by the conservatives, stayed in power, all might have been well; but almost at once he was ousted by Carranza, whose ten years of rule drenched the land in blood and crushed it under injustice—the most flagrant of which was the revival of the old anti-religious laws.

So the dark shadow of contemporary history threw its length athwart that day in August of 1913, the Feast of the Assumption, when you took your vows; for no member of the family could be present, so lawless were the times. Then, almost at once there came the shocking news that your father had been ousted from the control of his mines in Saltillo and been forced to flee; that your mother, with the younger children, was also in flight. Your anxiety must have been intense as you waited there in the novitiate, day after day, for news of them. Finally came word that they had escaped with their lives, and that was about all.

It was no wonder that you became ill. Anxiety and sorrow had brought on those interior ulcers which throughout your life were to cause such prolonged suffering. Yet we are told that you tried to conceal your illness, maintaining the gaiety and jests which had endeared you to all at El Llano, and even beginning your career as a teacher. Then into the novitiate began to come those tales of the horrible religious persecution being waged by the revolutionaries. Church property was being seized; priests were being tortured and killed.

Was it not about this time, Father Pro, that you began to hear the soft call audible only to the martyr; that you began to long for the opportunity of shedding your blood as a "witness" to Him? One night, not long thereafter, it must have seemed as though the opportunity had come: that dreadful summer night made hideous by the sound of shots and shouts, when a band of revolutionaries broke through the gates, galloped down the avenue, and invaded the hacienda, demanding the account books, breaking up furniture, looting the kitchens. But your time had not yet come. Quixotically they left off their depredations as suddenly as they had begun, riding away into the night.

But naturally that episode was enough for your superiors. The part of wisdom cautioned dispersal until the times should improve. It must have been a very sad day, that last at your beloved El Llano, as you and the other seminarians packed your few belongings, donned civilian clothes, and moved off in small groups, each to a designated billet. I don't know about the others, but you personally seemed to have moved from the frying pan into the fire! For no sooner had you reached the town of Zamora and the home of your fellow student, Rios, than the revolutionaries seized all the priests in town, tortured them, and threw them into prison. Yet it is evident that you actually enjoyed the excitement, Father Pro, as you passed under the noses of the bandit-army, disguised as a gay peon—a part you could play to perfection. In imminent danger of your lives, it was a relief to read that secret orders came from your superiors to take yourselves off to the larger town of Guadalajara, which, though also occupied by revolutionaries, because of its size promised greater safety.

How glad you must have been at last to reach it in your successful disguise after a hair-raising journey! You were far happier even than the others, for it was in Guadalajara that your mother had taken refuge, and now after the long, harrowing separation you would see her again, and the small brothers and sister. And even though they were reduced to great poverty, and your courageous mother forced to do menial work (she who had always enjoyed plenty and luxury), I think with joy of that reunion. All the Señora Josefa had been able to salvage from the wreck of the lovely home in Saltillo was a small image of the Sacred Heart. "I am glad, so glad," she told you, "to have had to leave everything for the sake of Christ, Our Lord." It was in that poor home which you visited every day that the good news finally came of the safety of your father in his remote exile.

But as the weeks passed and the net tightened around all religious, the Jesuit superiors, keenly conscious of their obligations to the dispersed seminarians of El Llano, determined to send them out of the country—and you've no idea, Father Pro, how glad I am that it was my own country which offered a refuge! I'm sorry that your visit here was so fraught with heartache at leaving your cherished, bleeding Mexico, your mother and the family, that you could barely have been happy in the United States. But I do know that the hospitable Jesuit novitiate at Los Gatos, California, which welcomed the young Mexicans, was a happier place for your sojourn there. And at least there must have been some satisfaction in once more being able to resume your studies in peace. My countrymen must have found you the most delightful of companions. For it is said that you were always the life of every gathering, with your guitar and mandolin, your jesting and songs. Ever since the days at El Llano, you had been gathering a reputation as a poet; and by now, the patriot player-poet was the star performer at every novitiate entertainment. But one can guess that when you were alone, you pondered the increasingly bad news from Mexico with a heavy heart and a deep despair of ever being able to return. The history of that time reads like a bad dream, Father Pro. Villa was ravaging the north; Zapata the south; persecution and bloodshed raged.

I can imagine how you longed to return, to pour out your blood for God and country. But still the hour for which you longed was not at hand. Instead of moving closer to Mexico, your destiny carried you thousands of miles farther away—to the land of your forefathers. The Jesuit superiors had deemed that Spain was the place for sixteen of the young Mexican seminarians to continue their studies. With heart pulling you to the south, you obeyed implicitly; and it was a blessing, Father Pro, that as you sailed eastward across the ocean, you could not then foresee that it would be eleven long years before you would again set foot on your native land.

As you later looked back upon them, those eleven years must have seemed kaleidoscopic, so many studies did you master, so many places did you touch. At Los Gatos, it had been the classics and teaching; at Granada it was philosophy for five years; back across the ocean again, but alas, not to Mexico but rather to Nicaragua, where for two years it was teaching; then again to Spain, to Barcelona, where it was theology for two years; then in 1924 to Enghien in Belgium for theology.

The first World War had come and gone. Carranza, assisted by Obregón, had seized the presidency of Mexico late in 1916, imposing upon the land that infamous Constitution of Queretaro, designed to destroy utterly the Church. Hundreds of priests had been exiled, religious vows were forbidden, all ecclesiastical property seized, and two thousand Catholic schools had been closed. By 1919 the policy had softened; but all through your long exile Mexico must have seemed forever to be either teetering on the verge of an abyss of bloodshed, or just staggering wearily out of one. How eagerly you must have fallen upon the long letters from your mother, devouring not alone the family news but the tidings of your poor, distracted country. Small wonder that the inner, physical suffering had increased proportionately with the tragedy of the picture. It is said that by sheer force of will you bore the pain uncomplainingly, even with humor, and never let your superiors guess it.

It is happy to reflect, Father Pro, that one great joy broke through the dark grey of those skies with the glory of a summer sunrise—the joy of your ordination as a priest, there in the establishment of the French Jesuits at Enghien, on August 31, 1925. You were thirty-four years old. Fourteen years had passed since that memorable retreat, begun in fierce resentment against the sons of Ignatius, and ending in your total embrace of the Society of Jesus. It had been a long preparation; you had been tried, and tried again, and not found wanting. Ignatius had a new son, of the caliber he most desired for his Society.

It was characteristic that you requested permission to devote the two months' holiday which followed to the workers, the miners above all, in Charleroi, that mining town on the Sambre in the Belgian "black country." As you went in and out of the mines, preaching the Christ of the worker, one can imagine that you told yourself this was the most ideal vacation of all. No one had ever guessed how often during the years your thoughts had turned back to the mines in Mexico and to the brave men whose risks and dangers you had shared as a boy.

Undoubtedly it was those strenuous days in Charleroi which brought to a crisis the long malady, a crisis so serious that your superiors could no longer be kept in the dark. You must have had to call upon all your powers of resignation when you were forced to capitulate and enter the Clinique St. Remi in Brussels, for an operation. It interfered most awkwardly with the completion of your studies in theology. And while the surgeons cut you open, not once but three times, they fortunately left your sense of humor unimpaired and while removing many other things, did not attempt to remove your funny bone. For apparently, you continued to afford endless merriment to the sad and the discouraged in the clinic. It is related that one operation, most painful, had to be endured without an anaesthetic; and that while it was in process, you occupied yourself in studying the Code of Canon Law. (Was there no lighter reading material at hand, Father Pro?) You had assured your superior: "I am not afraid of physical pain—'she' is such an old friend!" (Now I wonder why you gave pain the feminine gender, Father Pro? You hadn't yet met those pious old ladies of whom I reminded you in the first part of this letter. But I suppose Saint Paul would say you were justified.)

Perhaps all the terrible pain, all the suffering, were part of the preparation of the true martyr. When the end finally came in your glorious "witnessing," you did not flinch. Almost two thousand years before, neither had that other jester, Saint Lawrence, flinched.

It was in Brussels too, as though to complete a full cycle of suffering, that you bore the blow of your mother's death. I wept for you, Father Pro, when I read how this crushing news came as you lay there, trying to recover from the three operations. She, and you, had longed for the day when she could assist at a Mass celebrated by her son. . . . I have followed you through the long weeks at Hyères in the south of France, where you had been sent for recuperation, and where finally came the long awaited summons back to Mexico. It seems that your recuperation wasn't moving fast enough to satisfy the doctors (no wonder, with all the extra spiritual duties and corporal works of mercy you had voluntarily assumed), and it was deemed best to return you to your native land. Naturally, you suspected they were returning you to give you the quasi-pleasure of dying there!

So it was a joy to read that almost at once you began to "pick up," racing happily back to Enghien, then to Lourdes (there, you told yourself, Our Lady would surely help!) and then to St. Nazaire to take ship for Mexico on June 24, 1926.

And it surely seemed as though Our Lady had helped when even to your own surprise, you found that aboard the *Cuba* you could keep busy from morning till night at spiritual tasks which might normally be allotted to three priests—there was such a large passenger list, and you the only priest aboard. There was no time even to take the innumerable medicines which had been ordered; and apparently you did not even miss them!

Reckless with your body, you were just as reckless with

your skin, if you don't mind my saying so. For you knew perfectly well that by openly serving as a priest in all that throng, you could very easily be turned over to the authorities on landing in Mexico. Was not Calles in power? And had not Soviet Russia assured him that he not only completely understood the doctrines of Communism, but that he was also carrying them out perfectly? He had reintroduced the Constitution of 1917 which secularized all education, forbade all religion in the schools; outlawed all religious orders; enforced government supervision of all public worship. Just how would you, a returned Jesuit, stand in the eyes of the authorities? To my mind, your chances weren't worth a nickel, as the *Cuba* pulled into port there at Vera Cruz on July 7, 1926, and five hundred and twenty-five passengers debarked—any one of whom might have been a Communist.

I could have cheered when I read how you slipped in unnoticed—cheered, and recalled those lines of the poet: "This is my own, my native land!" The heart within you must surely have repeated them. And when on the very next day you were in the capital, Mexico City, it was surely the beginning of the most exciting part of your all too brief life. I would challenge any hero of history to offer a more exciting record packed into seventeen brief months: those dashing, adventurous, danger-fraught months which led up the path to martyrdom. They read like a great detective story. No "Who-Done-It?" (excuse the Americanism, Father Pro) was ever as thrilling. And now the born actor came into his own.

You could not have arrived at a more dramatic moment. Apart from the joy of finding your father safe and well in Mexico City (what a reunion that must have been—how many times had you not despaired of ever seeing him again!) and the young brother, Roberto, and the little sister, Ana Maria, with him, there was the dramatic news that Humberto, the other brother, was at that very moment in prison for upholding the principles to which your life was dedicated. On the larger stage, the drama revealed that Calles had only recently issued a manifesto increasing the proscriptions against the Church. The bishops had responded by the desperate means of decreeing an interdict to take effect within three weeks of your arrival. The Blessed Sacrament would be removed from all churches throughout the land; all priests would be prohibited from performing religious rites. The churches themselves would remain open—empty shells—for the worship of the public. The bishops would entrust them to God and to the faithful.

Of course this meant that any priest, during the three weeks preceding the interdict, would be worked overtime—in the confessional, at the Communion rail; in baptizing and marrying all eager to avail themselves of the Sacraments before the tragic withdrawal of the Church into the secret depths of the catacombs. Of this time it is related that, under the direction of your superiors, you labored day and night; and that Our Lady of Lourdes did not fail you. Miraculously you stood up under the sleepless, incessant program; and although you fainted twice in the confessional, I'm sure that by the end of that period, all the medicine bottles had been tossed away. Whatever odd moments there were must have gone to that visit to Humberto in prison, finally achieved after a dozen futile attempts, and to consultation with your superiors on a plan of action. Humberto's recital of his activities for the League of Defense and the Association of Mexican Catholic Youth, the cause of his arrest, had seemed like a clarion call to you. To keep alive the Faith, to save souls, to win souls for Christ while Satan strode the streets and lanes of Mexico, his Soviet-fashioned hands spreading sacrilege and dripping blood! That was your mission and the mission of the Jesuits. It could not have been more clearly defined.

We are told there were then 800,000 inhabitants of Mexico City. What a thrill you must have felt when it was determined that your apostolate should be right there in the capital, and right under the nose of Calles, whose beautiful palace, the Alcazar of Chapultepec, rose on its lovely wooded hill on the fringe of the city. So, under the persecution of Nero, had Peter and Paul labored at the Emperor's gates in Rome, in the year 64; so had Lawrence labored right beneath the nose of Valerian, in the year 258; and so had another Jesuit, Edmund Campion, performed his priestly duties right under the large nose of Elizabeth, in 1581. Miguel Pro, of our own time, was to follow faithfully in their footsteps, in the years 1926 and 1927.

You would confess the penitent; celebrate Mass and distribute the Holy Eucharist; baptize, marry, bury the faithful —in hidden, secret places—in whispers. Detection meant sure imprisonment and probable death. Clad in a dozen different disguises, you were to perform your priestly functions. The Christian soul, the martyr-soul, soared to the challenge. And the soul of the born actor responded with merriment to the opportunity.

It was significant, Father Pro, that you celebrated your last public Mass in the Jesuit church of the Holy Family, on the Feast of Saint Ignatius Loyola, July 31st, the day the interdict went into effect. This day also marked the beginning of the peaceful protest of the loyal Catholics of Mexico: their answer to Calles in a boycott restricting all nonessential spending. Theaters, restaurants, all luxuries were eschewed, and Calles fretted helplessly as business grew worse and worse and complaints poured in. Yet nothing seemed able to subdue his fixed determination to ruin the Church. It was really stupid of him, Father Pro; for the more he persecuted religion, all the more did the people reach out for it. Such a demonstration of faith in Mexico had never been seen before: the thousands of barefoot pilgrimages to the Shrine of Our Lady of Guadalupe; the millions who arose before dawn, all over Mexico, the old and crippled, the young and strong, to seek out the secret rendezvous where waited a priest with the Blessed Sacrament. Their numbers, their vivid faith, must have inspired you; I'm sure you inwardly vowed rather to die, than to fail them. And that was why, in the grey, pre-dawn light, at least three hundred persons a day received Holy Communion from your hands at those hidden "Eucharistic Stations" you had established all over Mexico City; why, on the First Friday, you gave Communion to at least twelve hundred.

I should have loved to have been at those services, Father Pro. I can imagine the thrill of rising quietly in the small hours, of stealing out into the dark streets; of finding the way somehow to the rendezvous, of approaching it with caution, looking to right and left for any of the ten thousand government spies employed by Calles; of feeling that at all costs, the "padre" must be protected. Of whispering the password, of entering breathlessly on tiptoe; of the hushed whispers, as people arrived, one by one—never in a group. Here was a great lady in a priceless mantilla, there an Indian with a huge Mexican sombrero. There followed the hushed expectant wait. Then suddenly into the room would come a young student, with rakish cap set at an angle over one eye, a foppish long cigarette holder dangling from his fingers—and lo, it would be you, Father Miguel Pro, of the Society of Jesus! Silently the Mass would begin. At the Consecration, no bell—but never were there more devout communicants. Their hearts with their Lord; their ears attuned for the slightest noise outside. It would be the Father who would be taken, not the faithful—so they must protect you at all costs.

Believe me, Father Pro, I myself have quaked at the fearful moment experienced by your "parishioners," when on that particular occasion one of the maids in the large hacienda rushed in to interrupt the Communion with the alarm: "The police are here!" As though I had been there, I can hear your whispered admonitions to the people to keep calm, to hide their religious emblems, and to disperse quickly into the various rooms of the mansion. I can see you hiding the Host in your breast; see you whip on the gay student's hat, insert a cigarette in the long holder, and debonairly greet the officers as they entered. Public worship going on here? Why, you never heard of anything so preposterous! A priest on the premises? Not any that you had seen. Accompany them through the house in their search? But certainly.

And even though you almost lost the game through pretending a knowledge of the house you did not in the least possess, they ended by thanking you and posting two of their number at the front door to prevent the exit of the hidden priest. A half hour later, you casually sauntered past this guard, explaining that you had business elsewhere, but would return to assist them further. They merely blinked their approval. It's delicious to reflect that the "business" which called you elsewhere was actually another Mass at the next station where the faithful waited. That completed, how amusing it is to think of your gay return to the two solemn guards at the hacienda, and your solicitous efforts to help them find that rascal of a hidden priest. It was simply too bad for Calles that he did not know there was a great actor in the ranks of the outlawed Jesuits.

But as the penal laws began to be enforced with ever greater severity, even your ingenuity must have been hard pressed.

How to find "stations" which would not arouse suspicion? We read that sometimes a half-completed building in the heart of the city would be utilized, as in the dark the faithful scrambled silently over beams and bins of concrete; or again that in a great modern office building they would kneel among the desks and filing cabinets.

Humberto had finally been released from prison; and returned to work just as avidly as before for the Mexican Catholic Youth Association. Was it he, or perhaps you, who dreamed up that famous "balloon barrage"? All we know is that one fine day, the people of Mexico City looked up and saw a mass of toy balloons floating above, which let fall upon the streets a flutter of printed matter, denouncing the government's attacks upon religion. The game was a huge success. Calles was furious, and the Pro family again under suspicion, although it was not then known that the "student" in the family was actually a priest.

Nevertheless you have probably not forgotten your arrest late that evening, and the riotous night you and the other suspects spent in prison. It is related that orders had come from Calles to give you all a most uncomfortable time; and so on that cold December night you were told to sleep outdoors in the breezy prison courtyard. You retaliated by making the night hideous for your jailors by singing at the top of your lungs and dancing about all night to keep warm. They must have been glad to see the last of you, and have particularly cautioned the irrepressible "student" to behave with less levity; to begin to realize that after all, he was no longer a child, but a grown man.

Yet now more than ever did suspicion center upon the house of Pro; and I think it most fortunate that when the next bevy of police arrived to make arrests, you shrewdly calculated what it would take to buy them off and were able to produce the money. But of course now you all knew that you must abandon a home together, and lose yourselves individually among relatives and friends. One can imagine your disappointment when your superiors, in their quite natural desire to preserve you, now decreed a period of hiding and inactivity; and whether you liked it or not, you had, temporarily, to subside. You could hardly blame your superiors as they watched the rising tide of persecution. For soon the Archbishop of Mexico would be arrested and exiled. Soon more than three hundred priests from all parts of the country would be imprisoned in Mexico City, two with their wrists broken because they had dared to celebrate Mass.

Not much later, five members of the Catholic Youth League would be tortured and shot. And on Good Friday, that horrible scene would be enacted which would be with you to your dying day, when the young president of the League, a typographer aged twenty-three, would be made to mock the Crucifixion, as from the hours of twelve to three he would hang suspended from a tree in the form of a cross—and mercifully shot at three o'clock.

How you prayed, in that seclusion, to be allowed to re-enter the lists! And only because you were so badly needed was permission finally granted. It would seem, Father Pro, that you emerged from that retreat with renewed zest and a thousand fresh ingenuities. I feel certain that you had devised several new disguises, grown a handsome moustache, and rehearsed many a new role to baffle the police. We know that the actor had increased his store of "props": the careless student's attire, the long cigarette holder and cane, the flower in the buttonhole, by the addition of a very handsome police dog. Who would suspect a Jesuit of going about with a pedigreed dog on a leash?

I forgive you for being convulsed over those pious old ladies, when I read that your next retreatants were a group of fifty taxi drivers—a class to whom I'm personally devoted and can't but feel had more need of your spiritual ministrations than the old ladies. They welcomed you as one of themselves, for after all, you could speak their language as well as you spoke that of the miners; and what a happy time you all had, hidden away there in a vacant lot behind a high fence, and discussing the Spiritual Exercises of Saint Ignatius. It seems that you were brash enough even then to take on eighty government employees. The risk was enough to make anyone's hair stand on end.

But risk was what you thrived on. Can one ever forget how you eluded those two spies who waited at the corner that night you emerged from a dwelling where you had been conducting a retreat? It took no time at all to realize they were following you, only waiting an opportune moment to seize you. But you had other ideas. What a bit of luck it was, Father Pro, that a taxicab happened along—and, on springing into it, to learn that the driver was a good Catholic. Looking back, you saw your pursuers following in another taxi. I should have been panic-stricken at such a moment; but you merely outlined a plan to your driver, and he collaborated. Swooping around a corner suddenly, he slowed down a second to permit you to jump out of the moving cab as he drove serenely on, as though you were still a passenger. Immediately the other cab rounded the corner, continuing in hot pursuit of the first. If the spies looked out at all, they would have seen a stranger leaning nonchalantly against a tree, hatless, and with a white shirt. They could have sworn that the man they pursued had worn a cap, and a black waistcoat. Imagine their surprise, when after a merry chase, they finally drew up alongside an empty cab! During those frantic times, you seemed to have a lot of fun, Father Pro. And while perhaps one shouldn't remind you, to play pranks on the police appears to have been your special joy.

I have laughed aloud over the ingenious means you took of displaying those propaganda "stickers," secretly printed by the Youth League, one of which would occasionally appear as though by magic even upon the private motorcar of Calles himself. It is related that, when sedately seated in a streetcar and unobserved by the other passengers, you somehow managed to stick them upon your own back. When you arose at your stop to walk gravely down the length of the car, all the passengers read the sticker and smiled at the poor innocent "professor" who had been the "victim" of such a hoax.

It is delightful to reflect that you could "sandwich in" this sort of play in the midst of danger, hairbreadth escapes, and your intense spiritual activities—for such a comic relief was needed, Father Pro. Perhaps you did not even mind that there was less and less time for sleep so long as there was time for an occasional laugh along that harrowing path which every day grew more tragic for the people of Mexico. For there were the poor, who by now had come to look upon you as their only friend, and whose plight in Mexico City wrung your heart. For these, you had become a beggar, daily increasing your dependents until finally at the end it is said that no less than ninety-eight families looked solely to you for food, lodging, and clothing. It is related that you were often seen in the streets with huge sacks of provisions on your back, begged for your poor from some friendly merchant. Apparently you didn't stop at merchants, for there is that amusing letter you wrote to your Provincial:

"People give me valuable objects to raffle: things worth ten piasters bring in forty. One day I was bearing off a bag—a lady's—extremely pretty (I mean the bag, not the lady!)."

You related that you had expected to get twenty-five piasters for it, but suddenly encountering a lady who was none too easy in her conscience, you sold her the bag for fifty, directing her to take the money herself to the hungry family who needed it. Thus several birds were killed with one stone. I wondered and wondered how you had come so to love the poor, Father Pro, and then one day I chanced upon a confidence you had once made to another: "Do you know where I got the little experience I have? Where I learned to love? It was in the Heart of Jesus."

But it was inevitable that as the crowded, terror-ridden months flew past, you should become more and more a marked man. Too many people in Mexico City were now familiar with the slim, elegant young man with the high forehead, the dark, intensely alive eyes, the laughing student who was forever popping up suddenly in the most unlikely places. Too many times had you eluded the police, joked your way out of a tight spot; and it was no longer funny to them. Reports had come to Calles that there was a disguised Jesuit at large in Mexico City, and a warrant had been issued for your arrest. Rather than quailing before it, there seems to be no doubt at all that an arrest was precisely what you wanted—after giving them first a merry chase. For someone has told us that you had "promised the saddest saints of Heaven to dance a *jarabe tapatio*" if the warrant out against you should succeed. I learned with great pleasure, Father Pro, that a *jarabe tapatio* is nothing less than a Mexican tap dance. I'm sure you kept your word and performed the same with skill and agility, for those "saddest saints"—and left them laughing. I only wish I could have seen it! And I think Saint Lawrence must have been right there, clapping.

This point of view, of course, would have been all Greek to Calles. One could not expect him who had embraced with such thoroughness the doctrines of Soviet Russia to understand such lines as these you wrote to your superiors:

"... the power of our enemies is great; they have money, arms, and lies, but it will fall .... Already the splendor of the Resurrection can be foreseen precisely because the darkness of the Passion is almost at its height. From all sides, news comes of outrages and vengeance; the victims are numerous, *the list of the martyrs grows every day. Oh, if I could only draw the lucky number!*"

Calles thought that death would be the worst punishment he could wreak upon you. And that's where you tricked him again, Father Pro. To your joy, you sensed that "the lucky number" would soon be coming up, and characteristically set about protecting others. It would be unjust, you felt, to embarrass by your presence in their homes any of the kind friends who up to this time had given you shelter. There was nothing for it but to rejoin your father and brothers; the Pros must face the music, but you prayed that the others would not be called upon to suffer for your apostolate.

It is a tribute both to your intellect and skill as an actor, Father Pro, that Calles, wanting to take you for those many long months, wanting to catch you red-handed at your work as a priest, was never able to do so for the simple reason that you could think faster than he; and that finally to get you, he had to resort to a trumped-up criminal charge whose roots were political. Even we poor ignorants in the United States (on Mexico's religious persecution, saving the Catholic press, our press was largely muzzled) knew that one fine morning in November, 1927, an attempt had been made upon the life of General Obregón. On his way to join President Calles at a bullfight, two bombs were thrown at his car. He escaped with only a scratch, but there were other victims; among them, one Nahum Ruiz, an occupant of the murder car which had been pursued and fired upon. Ruiz lingered for several days in the hospital before death finally claimed him.

Calles had immediately spread the story that the attempt on General Obregón's life was the work of the Catholics. General Obregón had his doubts; and looked upon the voluble Calles, his supposed friend, with a cold and fishy eye. He wondered. And the more he wondered, the more nervous grew Calles; the more determined to arrest someone, anyone, for the crime. Of course the true facts have never been revealed, but it would seem, Father Pro, that the idea had suddenly struck him that this would be an excellent way of getting rid of that troublesome Jesuit.

In any case, we do know that the police were set to guard the bed of the dying Ruiz, and to extract a confession from him. After his death, they rushed to Calles with a concoction it was hard for the Mexican people to swallow. You remember that they declared that the dying man had said: "Tell Father Miguel Pro-Juarez; Señor Humberto, his brother; and Señor Luis Segura Vilchis, to hide." The first was that impudent, troublesome Jesuit; the other two were leaders in the League of Catholic Youth, the very same organization which had released those impertinent balloons. The "statement" was precisely what Calles wanted; in fact, one might say, it looked as though it had been "made to order." Surely, these arrests would satisfy General Obregón!

It appears that after all, they didn't. He seems to have felt, quite rationally, that if any of you three had been implicated, it was an odd thing that you had lingered in Mexico City. There had been ample time to make an escape in the two days which elapsed before Ruiz died. But I'm far less concerned with what Obregón thought than with the outrage against the Pro family which followed. I can imagine that moment in your simple apartment whose whereabouts were supposedly unknown to the authorities, when you, Humberto, and Roberto, were suddenly awakened before dawn to see the room filled with armed police. They were amazed at your coolness. "Just a moment," you said, "until I can hear my brothers' confessions." And off you moved to a quiet corner to perform this last duty for those you loved, while the nervous police waited. For you knew this was the end, at least for yourself and Humberto.

What followed seems incredible in a country that, under Calles, was then trying to call itself a "democracy." But he had the Soviet conception of same. As awful as they were, Father Pro, one can somehow accept the idea of the filth and horrible discomfort of those underground dungeons into which you and Humberto were flung (although I'm very glad I wasn't called upon personally to accept them, Father Pro!), but where the mind bogs down utterly is on the stark fact that these prisoners of a "democratic" State, charged with the crime of attempted murder, were given no examination, no opportunity to make a statement, and no trial. You were simply taken out to the prison's picturesque patio and shot. This, under the "benevolent" Calles. But not before he had time to blazon the arrests in the newspapers, and to assemble a distinguished audience of all the top brass, newsmen and photographers, to witness his curious sense of justice. But nevertheless very definitely before Obregón had time to insist upon a trial. They let him know all about it after you were dead. (I have an idea that Calles caused you infinite amusement, Father Pro.)

And I hope you won't mind my saying that I get a certain amount of amusement myself out of your own behavior during the six uncomfortable days spent in those horrible dungeons. It is related that you shared your food with all, gave the warders your cigarettes (to my mind, the greatest heroism!) and succeeded in actually converting one of them before you died. You led the recitation of the rosary at the top of your voice for all the prisoners; gave them absolution through your prison bars; recited prayers and sang hymns—all ending with a "community sing" of the March of Saint Ignatius. This son of Ignatius was not relaxing his efforts one bit, even though he had only a few more days to live. I call it a thorough job, Father Pro.

One understands even more of Calles' motive in not bringing you to trial when one reads that, according to Mexican law, had you been tried and even found guilty, the worst punishment that could be inflicted was a mere imprisonment of twelve years. But that would not have suited his purposes. So he had Roberto Cruz, the prefect of police, release a story to the press that you had all confessed your guilt. This story was oddly at variance with those of two journalists who somehow had been able to penetrate the prison and see you. Two different newspapers quoted explicit denials of the crime, as made by each prisoner individually. The poor Mexican public must have been in a fine state of confusion. Obregón had sent his lawyer to the prison to state officially that he did not believe in the guilt of the prisoners, and that he hoped the trial would not be delayed. With excessive Latin politeness, the lawyer had been assured that the General's wishes would be respected; in fact that trial would take place the following day. What took place was not a trial but an assassination—held, so Cruz later declared, upon the explicit order of Calles.

But all this, you will tell me, is not important to you and to me. For you, the "lucky number" had at last come up; and I can imagine with what a light step you followed the gendarme who had been sent to conduct you from the dungeon. And how warmly you pressed your brothers' hands; with what a cheery voice you cried to the others: "Goodbye, my sons, my brothers!" And when the gendarme haltingly asked your pardon, with what warmth you threw your arm across his shoulder and said: "Not only do I pardon you, but I thank you!"

The soldiers who lined the patio, the generals and officers who sat on the dais, the newsmen and photographers who moved about, must have been struck by that quick, light step of the slim young man, not yet thirty-seven years old, as he approached the stockade at the far end, that sinister target. They must have marveled at the oddly happy light which suffused his face. So this was the long-hunted Jesuit–he who had outwitted Calles hundreds of times. What was he so happy about? Didn't he know he was about to be shot? Ah, yes; for now he was kneeling in prayer, his sensitive profile expressing a calmness and a dignity that were disturbing. Now again he was on his feet, facing the firing squad. But he was blessing them! With the priest's magnificent gesture of benediction, he was saying, "May God have mercy on you. May God bless you. With all my heart, I forgive my enemies." For thus had your Master taught you, Father Pro.

They did not bind your arms, nor blind your eyes. Somehow, even to them, it seemed quite unnecessary. Then, as the order was given, it is related that you flung wide your arms in the form of a cross, that gesture of love by which He died, and cried "*Viva Cristo Rey!*" as the shots rang out. "Long live Christ the King!" It was a glorious "testimony," a magnificent "witnessing." So died the patriot, player, poet, and martyr of Mexico. Even the generals looked away as the slim body sank to the ground. But one photographer did not look away. He clicked his camera just before you fell, and that is why that famous picture of you got abroad, Father Pro—the one which shows your own touching and very perfect "Imitation of Christ," with arms flung wide in a gesture of love. The Communists (will they never cease to be stupid?) released it as a warning to recalcitrant Catholics, but quickly discovered that it only served as an added inspiration to those fighting for their Faith.

So you were there in Heaven to receive your brother, the brave Humberto, when without flinching he followed you a few moments later. And the handsome young Luis Segura Vilchis, who was only twenty-three—he who had headed the League of Youth. At the last moment, the life of your younger brother, Roberto, had been spared.

"Do not weep," said your gentle old father when thousands poured out for the double funeral in a tribute which Calles himself could not have stopped: "Do not weep. For the priest was an apostle; and his brother, an angel."

It was the weeping poor particularly, those for whom you had begged and carried heavy burdens, who filed in thousands past your bier, pausing reverently to beseech your prayers for them—even as the poor of Rome, watching the fiery martyrdom of their protector, Saint Lawrence, had cried out to him to carry their petitions to Heaven.

When you and Saint Lawrence at last came face to face, bridging the sixteen hundred years which separated your martyrdoms as though they had been but a day, apart from your common love of the poor, your enjoyment of a jest, you would have found another point of congeniality. For the legends relate that while Rome was his beloved city of adoption, Lawrence actually came from Spain, as did your own ancestors. If he were living today, we would call him "one of our great young churchmen attached to the Vatican." He must have been very young when Pope Saint Sixtus appointed him custodian of all the goods and money of the Church, and entrusted him with the lovely delicate task of dispensing alms to the poor.

One thinks of the friendship which existed between those two: the ageing Pope and the lighthearted young Spaniard; and how Lawrence grieved when the Emperor Valerian's soldiers came to lead Sixtus to his martyrdom.

"Father," he cried, "whither goest thou without thy son? Holy Priest, dost thou fare hence without a deacon? It hath never been thy use to offer sacrifice without a minister. What therefor in me hath displeased thee, my father? Hast thou tried me and found me unworthy to be called thy son?"

But his heart lifted when the holy Pope replied:

"My son, I do not leave thee. Yet three days, and thou shalt follow me; the deacon behind the priest."

And just as Sixtus had foretold, after three days Saint Lawrence was led to his gridiron—but not before seeing that the poor were nicely cared for. With Lawrence, they had thoroughly enjoyed the joke on the grasping prefect of Rome, thwarted in taking what was not his; but their laughter was stilled when they heard the enraged prefect declare: "You mock me! I know you desire to die, in your madness and vanity. But you shall not die immediately, as you imagine. You shall die by inches."

And so, by inches, they watched him die over live coals; and as they wept, I think it was Saint Lawrence's desire to cheer them that led him to jest with his torturers, asking them to turn him over so he would be "well done" on both sides. He would make his exit on a laugh. He won the pagans who stood about, with this and with his courage. Moved by his fortitude, many became Christians at once; among them even several Roman senators.

And all this is why I am so very sure that you love Saint Lawrence, Father Pro, for it is certain that he loves you—jester, player, poet, and martyr of Mexico!

VII

To Father Delp of Germany,
Martyr and Mystic

concerning **SAINT LUCIAN**

Dear Father Delp:

It is only recently that I have met you; unhappily, not face to face, but only as one usually meets authors, in the lines they have written. Father, those lines have captivated me; so behold, now I am doing what I can never remember doing before —writing to an author, "sight unseen." Oh yes, I know that writing to authors one has not met personally is quite a common practice. But you'll agree, I think, that *one* author writing to *another* author is not so common—alas, for the egotism of our craft! Not that you shared a bit of it.

On doing the "Particular Examen" which you as a Jesuit and son of Saint Ignatius of Loyola would recommend for my disordered soul, I can't for the life of me discover why I've never written to authors before, for certainly one of my chief joys in life has come from reading their works. It may have been rank egotism; or again, because I was afraid they would snub me as the late Sigrid Undset (that glorious writer) once did in a face-to-face encounter.

Now you can see how you have worked upon me. Here you have me, right at the start, employed in the painful pursuit of examining my conscience. Could anyone doubt that you are a Jesuit?

Well, dear Father Delp, there's one thing certain, and that is that you are not going to snub me, no matter how awful I become in this letter, because, you see, I believe you to be a saint, a martyr of our own generation. And such nice people never snub anybody; particularly not sinners.

Perhaps right here I should tell you about Sigrid Undset, because it's not charitable to say she snubbed me without explaining that she had a perfectly good reason for doing so. (It's really terrible, the way you are working upon me.) Anyway, I attended a meeting in Washington once, at which she was a speaker. Now she had requested particularly that she would not be exposed to any questions from the press. As I was then, in a sense, a representative of the press and was brash enough to break through this prohibition and ask her a question, of course she had a perfect right to snub me.

If you are interested, I went up to her and asked her a question about that great book of hers, that great classic, *Kristin Lavransdatter*, which some years ago won the Nobel Prize. She gazed down upon me from her lofty eminence, with as superb a dignity as any of her own Norwegian fjords, and she said, quite finally: "I have forgotten Kristin." And off she moved in tremendous majesty. My face was very red. And my mouth open. It was like Shakespeare saying: "I have forgotten Hamlet."

Yet my job required me to write an account of her speech. Again I was brash, and sent it to her. Now, I considered it the most praise-making article I had ever written (for that's how I felt about her). I was very proud of it as propaganda for Sigrid. Imagine then how my jaw fell when I opened her acknowledgment containing these few simple, penned lines: "Mrs. Homan: Did I really appear as such a jackass?"

Perhaps now you can see, Father Delp, why since then I have not made it a practice to write to famous authors.

But you are different. As writers, neither Sigrid, a magnificent artist, nor I in my total inconsequence, can write as you wrote; for you see, Father Delp, I've just learned that you wrote those beautiful mystical passages of your book, *In the Face of Death*, with your hands tied. "So," you will say, "do most journalists write." But that will be in fun, for you know perfectly well that I mean you wrote with hands literally tied—with harsh chains. When I think of what a time I have—I who live in a free land (God bless it!) and with free hands—getting a few thoughts down on paper, and reflect upon you who lived in a slave land and had to write with bound hands, facing certain death, I am at your feet.

It was thus, in that terrible prison of Tegel in Germany, in 1945, when condemned by a Nazi court to hang, that you wrote down such thoughts as these:

"Many words, formerly familiar, have lost their sense and meaning on the positive height of existence at which I have now arrived. I don't even want to listen to them. All that, lies far below. I sit up here on my cliff, wondering whether, wondering when, someone will come to throw me off. Time has angels' wings, up here. One can hear them softly rustling, reticent and reverent before the absolute requirements of this altitude. Far below, there sounds the tossing and raging of a compressed storm. Too confined there, everything—too restricted for the real measurements and requirements. That was always my secret foreboding and opinion: everything was too confined. Among those words which here above retain their value, and reveal anew their meaning, are the words of the old prayers; but above all, the words which the Lord has taught us. Our Father...."

It was your beautiful exposition of the Our Father which first made me long to write you, to tell you how much it has meant to me. That, and the matter of your bound hands, which so reminded me of another martyr who died long ago—the lovable and loving Saint Lucian. He too was a scholar; and neither did he permit a mere matter of bondage to prevent him from continuing his functions as a priest, to use your own words, "in the face of death." Condemned to die, and while bound and chained down upon his back, did he not consecrate the Bread and Wine upon his breast, and dispense the Blessed Eucharist to the sorrowing Christians who bent over him? It is as though you and he had been brothers, so alike did you react to pagan bondage. Priests to the end; he with wrists bound, dispensing the Holy Bread, and you in similar wise, dispensing those exquisite spiritual reflections to sustain the friends who yet walked abroad but also in the fearsome shadow of death.

It has almost seemed as though Saint Lucian were whispering to me to go forth and learn more about my contemporary, Father Alfred Delp of the Society of Jesus, who gave his life for Christ in 1945, as Lucian gave his in the year 312.

So it happens that I have come to learn a little—not enough—about you: How you had been born there in Lampertheim, of Hesse in Germany, on September 15, 1907, the Feast of the Seven Sorrows of Our Lady. Because your birthplace lies in southwest Germany, near Bavaria, I first assumed that you had grown up in a Catholic atmosphere until I stumbled upon the fact that your father was not a Catholic. Evidently a man of positive ideas, there is an implication that he prevented your mother from practicing her religion and from bringing up her children as Catholics. I should love to know how it was, Father Delp, that you found your way back to your mother's Church—and apparently brought her along with you. Surely, no matter what were the family circumstances, you had absorbed from this loved mother the Catholic spirit which was her birthright. Later, a brother and a sister were also converted, so you four were at last of one faith—a great happiness for you, only marred by the attitude of your father to whom you were devoted.

As I write this letter, I am informed that happily he still lives in Lampertheim (as do your mother, brother and sister) and grieves over the fact that you ever became a Jesuit. One of your last messages to your friends, written with difficulty by the hands that were bound, reads:

"God protect you! Help my aged parents through these difficult days; and keep them otherwise a little in your care. ... To everyone, the Lord God's merciful protection!"

One can imagine then, the difficulties you must have met with that beloved father, when at nineteen, after attending the public school in Lampertheim, you determined to join the Society of Jesus. It was April of 1926, we learn, when you entered the Jesuit novitiate of Pullach, near Munich, and with that famous thoroughness of the Jesuit training, it was June 24, 1937, before you were finally ordained. On that happy day, did you guess, I wonder, that, after so many years of preparation, you would not be granted even a full eight years to work among men as a Jesuit?

One can easily recall how that year of 1937 was full of ominous portents, even to us here in America. The very air trembled with fear of war. The towering shadow of Hitler overhung all Europe; and if we here occasionally shivered under its chill, how much more so must you have felt it, there in the country he had molded into a unit that fitted nicely right into the palm of his hand. As an intellectual, you must frequently have paused and wondered—paused and prayed—for the land you loved as dearly as any patriot ever loved his country. You were not quite thirty years old on that day of ordination in 1937, but it is evident that some time before you had determined on your favorite study, sociology—and sought the permission of your superiors to devote much of your future energies to sociological problems.

It was, Father Delp, as though from the seclusion of the novitiate you had been watching the progress of National Socialism in Germany, and observing that while it superficially improved the condition of the worker, it increasingly ignored God; setting up instead that modern heresy, worship of the State. That, you knew, could only end ultimately in disaster to the worker, and to the world. Christianity, the great force which had always combatted the enslavement of man; had taught the equality of man; maintained the dignity of the individual against all comers; had taught the love of Christ for man and of man for Christ–was being challenged, defied. The principles of National Socialism were not the principles to sustain a threatened Christianity. You must, as a Jesuit and a German, see what you could do about it!

So it seems quite natural that closely after ordination, the scholar, Alfred Delp, began to write upon sociological problems for the Jesuit publication, *Stimmen der Zeit*, and that very shortly he had become its sociological editor. And it was the articles which began to flow from your brilliant pen, expounding eloquently as they did the social doctrines of Christianity, which forged the link in the tragic but glorious chain which led you to martyrdom. For it was these articles, we are told, that attracted the attention of Count Helmut von Moltke –he who was later to be tried with you, and sentenced to death at your side.

How much I have thought upon that amazing figure, Father Delp. We know him as a Lutheran, the great leader of the Resistance Movement in Germany during the Hitler years, the man who early determined that only a revival of Christian principles would save Germany. It is fascinating to reflect on the small group of men, trusted and true, whom he gathered about him, and of the secret meetings which were held at his famous castle of Kraisau. Of this group, comprised of Catholics, Protestants, leftists and rightists, we know that at least two were priests, Jesuits both: yourself, and your Provincial, Father August Roesch. And that of the two, you were the first to join the courageous movement.

It would appear, Father Delp, that because of your articles you were, from the start, logically destined to form a part of this movement. Von Moltke, foreseeing the eventual fall of Hitler and National Socialism, the collapse of one order and the necessity to rebuild anew, was creating a plan for the new order, built upon the old Christian ideals of the German people. With a plan in readiness, he felt he could forestall for his country a long period of chaos; and so he endeavored to draw into the movement experts in the various fields in which government functions. From your expressed views, you were the ideal planner in the sociological field.

It appears from the record that you did not hesitate to embark on this dangerous, secret undertaking; in fact, that you lost no time in volunteering your services after securing the permission of Father Roesch, then the Jesuit Provincial for the Bavarian Province with headquarters in Munich. It was, as you recall, the spring of 1942. World War II was near completion of its third death-strewn year. Hitler had annexed Poland, Estonia, Latvia, Lithuania, Karelia, Bessarabia; had laid siege to Moscow, and soon was to besiege Stalingrad. A few months previously, there had been added to his long list of opponents the United States of America. With what fervor you threw yourself into the Resistance. To do so was treason to your government. Not to do so would have been treason to God.

To many in my own land who watched the brutalities of Hitler from afar, who made unstinting sacrifice to defeat him, who sent their sons to die in the struggle, and who concomitantly quite often denounced the whole German race for permitting such a monster to govern, I would like to repeat something you wrote there in prison, in that beautiful treatise on the Our Father:

"I speak of the guilt which belongs to our daily life. That we are guilty because we have disappointed and failed; and that we are guilty because we are living at a certain time and hour of history, and permit what is happening. . . . Our generation is a guilty generation, guilty in a very great measure."

That you and many others believed this, and sacrificed your lives to prove it and to restore Germany's soul, should never be forgotten.

For this had you thrown yourself with ardor into the Von Moltke group, laboring ceaselessly, compiling documents and arguments for a new social order based on Christian justice and the Papal Encyclicals; risking your neck in hundreds of secret rendezvous and missions. As Hitler's star began to fall, those perilous days became even more perilous, with the net tightening about the home front to exterminate all hidden opposition. There was no open opposition—machine guns could speak with such rapidity!

The mixed group of all faiths and political shades which formed the "Kraisauer Circle," named for Count von Moltke's castle of Kraisau, worked quietly but feverishly. Papers, plans, blueprints began to accumulate; greatest caution was taken to hide these where they would not be discovered. About a year ago, Father Delp, there appeared in our great magazine, *The Sign,* an article on the "Forgotten Builders of New Germany," by Anthony B. Atar—and in it I read of those secret meetings. Thus I can picture you, the quiet young man with the serious face which bore that unmistakable withdrawn expression of the true mystic, making your way to the rendezvous as the

Gestapo patrolled the streets. The conspirators went alone, never in a group, each one arriving inconspicuously.

Not all the meetings were held at the castle but, as you recall, many in Berlin, in that apparently innocent, normal garage which held a secret room at the top. The exterior of the building gave no sign of its existence. Possibly disguised as a mechanic, you entered from the street, and first making sure you had not been followed, made your way to that secret stair in the rear which led to the conference room. There you would greet the others with the password, "*Grüss Gott*," the "God bless you" which was the Circle's substitute for "*Heil Hitler*." And there, Mr. Atar has told us, Count von Moltke would himself prepare hot soup and scrambled eggs for the group. Around that simple table, what vast plans were made! The meeting over, participants left quietly, one by one. Each knew he was risking his life. At any moment, the Gestapo, so expert at discovering secret meetings, might surround the garage.

We are told that to prepare for such an eventuality, the meetings would always begin with conversation on a general subject, quite remote from the topic all had in mind. Each would contribute his remarks, so that in case of surprise by the Gestapo, each could repeat with truth what had been discussed and no report would be at variance with another.

It is now well known that through two nerve-wracking, strenuous years, you and Father Roesch worked indefatigably in the Circle's efforts to save victims from concentration camps, to hide those whom the Gestapo sought, to keep up the morale of the Resistance, to spread spiritual tracts and prayers, to smuggle out money and religious supplies to the clergy in German-occupied Poland, France, and Hungary. It was a great work, Father Delp, one which wins all our admiration of the courage of those who dauntlessly carried it forward.

Father Roesch told Mr. Atar that in the latter stages he was never able to spend two nights in succession in the same place. But I think that the joy of saving the persecuted, of succoring so many in distress, of spreading the word of God where it was most needed, and of planning a Christian rebirth for your beloved Germany, gave you a certain miraculous strength, and the ability to forget fatigue when carrying out those prodigious assignments.

When so much good was being accomplished, how tragic must have seemed the news which broke in January of 1944. Count von Moltke had been arrested. Somehow they had caught up with him. Who would be next? It was only a matter of time.

How you must have prayed for that brave leader who loved Germany and who had daily risked death to restore it to Christ. In the opinion of Father Roesch, you and von Moltke were the two great heroes of the Circle. But apparently his arrest did not stop you and Father Roesch, and many of the others. The work went on; on, that is, until that sultry day in June of 1944, the famous June 20th, when at last someone had the courage to try to kill Hitler. But neither you nor Father Roesch had any connection whatever with the attempt. Indeed, later at your trial, you were completely exonerated of any connection with it. But of course you knew, the minute it happened, that the net would close tighter than ever, that not a soul in Berlin would go unwatched.

As day followed day, there were increasing arrests; and finally it was disclosed that many hidden documents had been discovered, implicating members of the Circle. You knew your time was short—but you also knew that you had "fought the good fight." So it was that, at the end of July, 1944, a little more than a month after the attempt had been made on the life of the man who had brought physical and moral destruction to his own people, they came to take you. It was in your own church. The accounts do not relate just how you were taken, Father Delp; but knowing how close you lived to God, it would seem certain that they came upon you when you were at prayer.

One can only guess how terrible was that long incarceration in the prison of Tegel, in Berlin; most of it in solitary confinement which endured more than five months up to the time of your trial. But among your papers written with the bound hands, one comes upon a farewell to your friends, and this reference:

"Those whom I have hurt, may they pardon me. I have expiated. Those to whom I was untrue and false, may they pardon me. I have expiated. Those to whom I was arrogant, proud, and hardhearted, may they pardon me. I have expiated. Oh yes, in those hours in the cellar, in those hours of the chained hands, body and soul—there, much was shattered. There, much has been burned out that was not worthy enough, or of any value."

Dear Father Delp, how dreadful it all must have been—the cruelty, probable torture, filth and physical discomfort, hunger and thirst. Worst of all, the utter loneliness. As the horrible days and sleepless nights melted into one another, as Christmas came and went (Christmas in that cellar!) and January approached, you must have prayed that the Nazi trial, that mockery of justice, would come soon. That they would get it over with, quickly. Then you learned that poor Count von Moltke who had been one year in prison would stand trial with you. And that there would be other defendants.

Those momentous days of January 9th and 10th, 1945, when you two faced the Nazi court, come to us vividly through your own words. But even without them, it was generally known at that time that Dr. Freisler, the head of the

"People's Court" which tried you, hated the Jesuits. "The man is smart, nervous, vain, and presumptuous," you wrote. "He plays a performance, and his antagonist must be defeated." After publicly and thoroughly insulting the Jesuits, after accusing you of treason against the State for plotting a re-Christianized Germany, he easily won his convictions—you and Von Moltke. The sentence was death by hanging.

Then with terrifying suddenness, the judgment of God fell upon him who had judged you. Dr. Freisler was blown to bits in an air raid which struck Berlin within twenty-four hours. Of the trial you wrote: "Everything was finished as soon as it began. One is not a human being . . . just an object; and everything under an inflated threadbareness of legal forms and phrases. Shortly before, I had read in Plato: 'That is the greatest wrong, which is accomplished in the form of right.' . . . Our real transgression and crime is our heresy against the dogma, the Third Reich."

But of all the other defendants at that mock trial, Father Delp, there is one in whom I am particularly interested. It is that one to whom you refer in the farewell message to your friends:

"The state of affairs of Gerstenmeier is . . . much worse than mine. Being a Protestant minister from whom usefulness is expected shortly (as he himself has told me), he was declared a vague theorist, and then everything else was overlooked. . . . With this, I'm not saying anything against Gerstenmeier. He is a fine, deeply religious man, and with all my heart, I do not begrudge him his life. He will still do much good."

From these lines it becomes obvious that you considered it far better to die than to live in the service of the Nazi State. Probably the Reverend Gerstenmeier thought so too. In any case, I hope that he did not have to function long as a tool of the Nazis—for you see, Father Delp, I have taken a great fancy to him. It is not alone that he possessed the courage to work with Von Moltke, with you and Father Roesch, but that I was told by an excellent authority that the reason we have your beautiful writings, penned in bondage, is because "a Protestant minister spirited them out of Father Delp's cell in the prison of Tegel." I should like very much to learn that it was Dr. Gerstenmeier. It is heart warming to think that a Protestant minister preserved these most Catholic and mystical meditations. It is matter for rejoicing that as a result of common suffering, a new spirit of cooperation has developed between Catholic and Protestant in Germany, which has united more closely than ever before, those who follow Christ.

Whoever it was who connived to spirit your messages out from that damp, dark cellar, into the light and into the hands of the friends you so greatly loved and missed, the occasion must have been one of the few human consolations during the slow minutes which ticked by in the course of the three weeks which passed before you went forth to die. The great risk taken by that minister was not only a tribute to you but to what you had written. He must have considered your spiritual meditations treasures to be preserved at all costs, even that of his own skin. How deeply grateful all of us who have read your thoughts "in the face of death" are to him.

These were the hours when you rested, high on that elevation you described in your words on prayer. It is evident that you had hoped to die immediately after sentence had been passed, and that your return to Tegel with Von Moltke puzzled you. Did your Lord not desire the sacrifice after all? Had it all been but a testing? Would there be a reprieve? You did not know. Dear Father Delp, you only waited and prayed to learn His will. "I sit often here before the Lord, and look at Him questioningly," you wrote with unconscious pathos.

You must have felt even more puzzled when news reached you toward the end of January that they had executed Von Moltke. Would your turn never come? Meantime, the exquisite meditations continued, and in them there are glimpses of the saint-sociologist. "Give us this day our daily bread," is to be interpreted as prayer for actual bread to sustain us. The Father expects us to ask Him for the daily, human necessities, as He does for spiritual gifts:

"Bread is a real anxiety to man which passes before the sight of God.... One must have been hungry once.... One must have experienced once an unexpected piece of bread coming like a grace from Heaven... to learn again the reverence for bread, and man's anxiety about it. As long as men hunger and lack the daily bread, so long one will preach in vain to them about the Kingdom of God; and also about the earthly kingdom.... It is very important that the anxiety about bread be taken on and mastered by the right people. Man must know that our bread, be it ever so plentiful and sure each day, is given us from the Eternal Hand of God.

"We do not ask for the full barn and well-filled pantries, but for our daily bread. The insecurity and risk of human life echoes in this prayer: life proves itself in trust, and not in security.... Whoever undertakes it thus, to him things will come again and again, because he has a secret pact with the Lord. Bread is important and sacred, but not bread alone sustains man. That, we all realize anew, who in the era of great plenty have suffered the second war, and for the second time the great need of bread. Bread is important; freedom is more important; but most important are unbroken loyalty and unbetrayed worship."

Immediately upon reading these thoughts, Father Delp, I think again of the early martyr of whom you so remind me:

Saint Lucian, who with bound hands consecrated the Holy Bread upon his breast. How well he understood what you meant, if he looked down from Heaven upon your prison during those last days, and saw you trace with difficulty, the chain cutting your wrists, those lines about the trial:

"At the passing of the sentence too, I was inwardly as little concerned as I had been during the two days of the trial. For I had the Most Holy with me, those two days; and before the ride to hear sentence passed, I . . . received the Food as the last nourishment. Thus, I wanted to be prepared; but I am still waiting."

That long wait must indeed have been the greatest of all your trials, Father Delp. One is slightly comforted when one reads that your beloved sister was permitted to visit you in prison. How grief-stricken were those hearts at home in Lampertheim; and above all, your father who could not understand why you had voluntarily brought all this upon yourself. If you had only not become a Jesuit, none of this would be as it was. Yet you would have liked to continue being a Jesuit for many years.

"Sometimes," you wrote, "melancholy takes possession of me, when I think of all that I had wanted to do. For only now, after all this, have I become really human, free inwardly, and much more genuine and real, more actual than before. Only now can the eye adjust itself to all dimensions and all perspectives. The abridgment and the stunted growth are being removed. But those who remain behind!"

Then was the priest in you crying out to be allowed to remain, to give them the wisdom and the secret peace which had come to you there on that high cliff, where "time had angels' wings, and one could hear them softly rustling, reticent and reverent before the absolute requirements of this altitude." Yet was your humility touching. "I hope I remain up here free from dizziness, and don't plunge down again," you confided in that last farewell.

As with all saints and martyrs, you had found the way to the cliff not easy. For it was the Way of the Cross. Calvary too was a summit. To reach it, He had carried His Cross up a steep grade. Climbing all the time with that great load upon His shoulders, how hot and dusty was the way. As He strained under the load, He must have had to swerve here and there, to avoid the boulders and the hollows—and all the time the pebbles and sharp stones cut His feet. It was constantly uphill. And so it was to your cliff, whither you had been wending your way ever since you had entered at nineteen the novitiate of Pullach. "The way to my cliff here," you wrote, "through how many hours of weakness and want did it not lead! Hours of dejection, doubt; and not knowing where to turn. . . . For the hours of temptation no one escapes."

But on the way up that steep incline, you had found the answer. "Man is in need of superhuman strength and power. When his connections with the real supernatural have been severed, he begins to dream of grandeur, or to make strange gods for himself—things, achievements, people, rank. I know how that is. I have dreamed and longed for, and loved and labored; and in reality all this was but a song of longing for the Final and Unchanging.

"With dreams and idols, man does not progress. He continually finds himself banished and given over to the limits and insufficiencies of creature-hood. That also, I experienced. All of a sudden, everything falls apart, and one holds the broken pieces in one's hands, where one believed one was holding full tankards. How one begins to realize that instead of the singing of an heroic song, one only whimpers and groans! Man, alone, can do nothing. . . . For man to be in God's grace, and the world in God's order: that is the Kingdom of God, the conquering of human need through God's fullness, the bursting of human limits through God's strength, the restraining of human wildness through God's discipline—all that is the Kingdom of God."

There, high on your cliff with bound hands, you were experiencing it. And beautifully, the utter dependence upon God had not in the least mitigated your love of friends and country; but rather only deepened it.

"Oh, my friends, that the hour did not strike again and the day did not dawn again, on which we could associate openly and freely for the word and work toward which we grew inwardly. Remain true to the quiet command, which inwardly called us again and again. Continue to love this nation, which has become in its soul so lonely, so betrayed, so helpless, and fundamentally so desolate and perplexed in spite of all the marching and declamations of certainty....

"The self-centered man ... is a creature without grace, and his way through the world will always be without grace and mercy. Permanently he works destruction for himself and others. He remains, in spite of his Promethean declamations, a failure in all things, tasks and problems. That is the key to the history of the recent epoch which did not succeed in accomplishing any of the needed and urgent tasks before it.

"The order of human living is so arranged that it needs something to worship. If the real center is moved or hidden, something else will be put in its place and falsely coerce worship.... These fakes are more exacting and pitiless than the Living God. They know nothing of the refinement of waiting patiently, of wooing freely, of the call of grace, of the blessed meeting. They only know demands, force, might, threats, and destruction. Woe to those who are different!

"So then, farewell. My crime is that I believed in Germany, even beyond an hour of need and night. That I did not believe in that arrogant tri-unity of pride and force; and that I did this as a Catholic and a Jesuit. . . . Germany beyond today is an ever self-renewing reality: Christianity and the Church as the secret longing, the bracing and healing strength of this country and nation; the Jesuit Society, as the home of men of character, whom one hates because one does not understand them in their free bondage, or because one fears them as a rebuke and a question in one's own pathetic bondage."

Then, Father Delp, one can see you raising those Jesuit hands:

"And so I will do at the end what I have so often done with my bound hands; and what I will do ever more lovingly and oftener, as long as I am permitted to breathe: Bless. Bless land and people; bless this beloved German nation in its need and torment. Bless the Church that the fountains within her may flow clearer and brighter. Bless the Society, that it may remain genuine and full of character and free; true to itself through the unselfish faithfulness to all things genuine and to all missions. Bless the people whom I have wronged. Bless everyone who was good to me; often too good!"

At length in those exquisite thoughts, dear Father Delp, we arrive at the spirit of the true martyr—of one who, in great humility, desired deeply to be, through his death, a "witness" for Christ. "I also ask the friends not to mourn, but to pray for me; and to help me as long as I need help; and to be certain afterwards that I was *sacrificed*—not slain. . . . Some day, others shall live better and happier, because we died. . . . If through one man, a bit more love and kindness, a bit more light and truth were in the world, his life has had a reason."

And finally we come upon the veritable, undeniable mark of the true martyr—forgiveness.

"The inner worldly guilt must disappear . . . so that the world can breathe freely, off and on. This means for us the sacrifice of all bitterness and animosity toward those men who have treated us thus. I am not angry at them; not even at the great clown of German justice. I feel terribly sorry for them all; and still more so for the people who handed themselves and their immortal souls over to them."

Now at last the bound hands were quiet. The writing ceased. Now the hands occupied themselves solely by clasping in prayer. It was very quiet, up there on the cliff when they came to take you—and hang you. It was February 2, 1945. . . .

This, my first letter to a great modern author, is drawing to a close. Sometimes I dream dreams, Father Delp, which though perhaps quite impossible of fulfilment, bring me much happiness. Such a dream has been born of the reflections you wrote "in the face of death"; wrote with bound hands as Saint Lucian long ago consecrated the Sacred Host. Now because he too was a great writer and editor, he must admire not only those written meditations, but also all you did as sociological editor of *Stimmen der Zeit,* which laid the path for the great crusade to re-Christianize Germany. I'm thinking of him as one born in the third century, in Samosata, of Christian parents, whose writings became famous, and particularly his editorship of the Greek Old Testament which he revised according to the Hebrew text. When he lay there in Nicomedia, bound down upon his back, they thought he would renounce Christ if they offered him only food prepared for pagan sacrifice. Lucian refused it, so they let him starve. But he did not starve, for he had a Food which sustained him, and which they could not comprehend. So they tortured him to death.

With these matters in mind about you, and about him—and with the open confession that I've always had a great weakness for editors (a particularly nice class, I hope you'll agree,

Father Delp) perhaps you will understand my new and fabulous dream. Could I, do you suppose, one day have the great pleasure of quietly "sitting in," on an editorial conference between you and Saint Lucian? (Sigrid Undset will tell you that I am nothing if not brash, Father Delp.)

VIII

To Saint Sebastian,
Protector against the Plague

concerning BISHOP BARROSO OF SPAIN

Dear Saint Sebastian:

From the time I was little, I have loved you, meeting you so frequently as artists have painted you—a handsome young man helplessly bound, your poor body pierced everywhere with the cruel arrows shot by the archers of the Emperor Diocletian. And always I have wanted to know you better. Then one day, on my first visit to Rome several years ago, I had the good fortune to visit your wonderful church, the ancient basilica of San Sebastiano; and there in its lovely dimness you seemed very near. I told you I would come back, some day.

But in all this time it was only the other day that I came to know you as the great protector against the plague, and learned that in its recurrence at intervals throughout history, recourse to you by the faithful has saved many from this dreadful scourge. There was the plague that decimated Rome in the year 680; another that scourged Milan in 1575; and still another which laid waste to Lisbon in 1599. In all these, the stricken attested again and again that they had been miraculously saved from death by the intervention of Saint Sebastian.

So now I am writing you urgently at a time when the worst plague in history is sweeping the world, to ask you to save us. It is truly a black plague, Saint Sebastian, this diabolical infection called Communism. It is not a city that I ask you to save—it is the world. For those of us who know you feel that this plague above all others you will want to arrest, since its purpose is to destroy the Kingdom of Christ upon earth which you died gloriously to preserve. That was in the year 286.

Of course you know about the millions who, some sixteen hundred years later, have been dying for the same cause in this, our Second Age of Martyrdom. Wherever Soviet Russia has spread the germ of this deadly plague, multitudes of martyrs have been going to torture and death with the name of Christ on their lips.

It is said—but you will know better than I—that the infection first appeared in the doctrines of Karl Marx of Germany, and quickly spread to Russia where the germ was fostered by Lenin who, agreeing that "religion is the opium of the people," bent his efforts on the destruction of the Kingdom of Christ. We first began to hear of it shortly after World War I. Its incubation having been carefully fostered, not long thereafter it was despatched by Russia to Mexico, where it created endless havoc. Stealthily and insidiously it seeped at the same time into my own country, the United States; and a short time later was disseminated with appalling results in Spain, where it became the veritable Black Death. Since then, it has attacked most of Europe and the East. It is time that we began praying to you, Saint Sebastian! It was time, long ago.

I believe that it is a matter of history, that Lenin, in planning the conquest of Europe by Communism, designed a campaign to start at the Eastern and Western extremities—Russia and Spain—and that from these ends, the hands of Communism would play Europe like a vast accordion, compressing it in its grasp.

You will remember that Spain was the first foreign soil upon which it wreaked its most persistent destruction; and it is curious to reflect, Saint Sebastian, that out of Spain, during

World War I, had come a physical plague known as the Spanish influenza which did indeed spread a veritable black death over much of the globe. Strange, that this infinitely worse spiritual plague should attack Spain so violently in the years 1936 to 1939. Those were the years when modern Christian martyrs in that basically Christian land died by the thousands at the hands of those infected—died as you did, because they believed in Jesus Christ.

Among all these there was one to whom you must feel particularly drawn, not only because the manner of his martyrdom was not unlike your own, but because his persistence in teaching the doctrine of Christ in the face of those determined upon its destruction was very like your own persistence under similar circumstances. I think of him so often, Saint Sebastian, in these days when the Communist accordion, emitting the dissonance of hell, is heard far and wide across the globe, when the Western powers stand as the sole bulwark to prevent the collapse of Christian civilization. He is (as no doubt by this time you have guessed) His Excellency, Bishop Florentino Asensio Barroso, late Bishop of Barbastro. That does seem a long title for so simple and so humble a man; undoubtedly you know him in Heaven by a name much simpler and more endearing.

Brave and unflinching in his "testimony" to the end, you must have been very glad to welcome him, Saint Sebastian. For when in 1936 the plague-infected Communists heartlessly left him there to bleed to death in the cemetery of Barbastro, you would have recalled how the pagan archers had left you to bleed to death on the Campus Martius in the year 286. And when he had worked feverishly and openly to spread Christian doctrine throughout a diocese already riddled with the plague before he ever set foot in it, when he courageously issued his pastoral letters calling all men back to the feet of Christ, you would have remembered how your own martyrdom had come about because you openly and constantly exhorted the Christians to stand firm in their belief against the power of pagan Rome bent upon destroying it.

I think of Bishop Barroso of Spain now standing at your side, and with us, asking you, one of the greatest of all the martyrs, to intervene with the Father to save the world from that blackest of plagues called Communism. For Florentino Barroso saw it wreaking havoc in one of the ugliest of all its very ugly phases. And now Christian Spain, having thrown off its Red domination, has come to revere him popularly as a saint and a martyr, and is promoting the cause for his beatification by the Church. I wish you would tell him, Saint Sebastian, that those of us who know him here, are praying for that also.

Only recently have we begun to learn something about his life. In these days, it is good for us to know about our modern martyrs, Saint Sebastian. Because he carried his utter simplicity and humility into the high honors thrust upon him, we find Bishop Barroso particularly appealing.

It is absorbing to reflect how often Our Lord selects as shepherds of His flock the simple ones of earth. Who, for instance, would have dreamed that the little son born on October 16, 1877, to Don Jacinto Asensio and Doña Gabina Barroso, the humble shopkeeper and his wife of the town of Villasexmir in Spain, would one day be consecrated Bishop of Barbastro? He was one of nine children; and of the six who survived, second to the youngest. Probably if at that time such a prophecy had been made to his mother, she would have dropped the infant out of sheer awe. For the parents were extremely religious.

It was a home in which the rosary was recited daily. And it is lovely to think, Saint Sebastian, of those days in Christian Spain, when the church bells rang out at the consecration of every Mass and the Barroso family, when not in church themselves, would drop whatever task was at hand and silently worship during those moments.

Florentino had been born on the feast day of the great Archangel Raphael—he who is known as "the Angel of Joy"—and indeed, Saint Sebastian, I think that Raphael blessed him with the gift of joy on that day; because humor was so generously mingled in a nature that was essentially spiritual. Later, when serving a wide-flung parish which required much traveling, he refused the offer of a horse, saying that he preferred to travel "on the horse of Saint Francis." And off he would go happily on foot. People relate that he was quick to see his own failings, and to laugh heartily at his own mistakes.

Although born in Villasexmir, he actually grew up in Villavieja where the family had moved when he was three years old. In those growing years, two marked characteristics developed: his ability as a student, and his early call to the priesthood. In that religious family, he was not the only one. An older brother, Cipriano, had entered the Augustinian Order; and a sister, Lucia, had determined to enter a convent. It is said that the young Florentino played at being a priest, with little Lucia as his "congregation." And it was very shortly after he received his first Holy Communion, at the age of ten, that he knew what God wanted of him. He must struggle every way, in that poor family, to obtain an education for the priesthood.

It was only accomplished, Saint Sebastian, through arduous study; first at the Latin school which he completed in the unusually short space of two years, with his good mother constantly worrying about his health as he took no time for play. Too young to enter the Augustinian novitiate where his brother Cipriano had been trained, on his splendid record he was accepted as a student of philosophy at the seminary of

Valladolid; and from then on, he began winning scholarships.

There in the seminary he devoted himself to study and prayer; and remembering always the family rosary which had been recited daily at home, he became a participant in the perpetual rosary, reciting his share every night in the chapel from half-past eleven to midnight—which, considering the seminarians' early rising hour could not have given him very much time for sleep. Fellow students were later to recall that somehow, among all those youths, Florentino had stood out as "someone, who some day, will become something." But I suppose they never dreamed, Saint Sebastian, that the "something" would be a martyr of their own generation.

He was only twenty-four when, in 1901, he was ordained to the priesthood; and by special dispensation, since he was a few months younger than the normal age requirement. Ever since he had been ten, he had worked so hard, Saint Sebastian, to answer the call of his Lord. Surely feet, weighted as his were with poverty and difficulties, never ran faster to attain that goal. Naturally, he celebrated his first Mass at home, in the little church of Villavieja, and in the joyful presence of his aged parents; his brother, the Augustinian priest, and the rest of the family. Now at last Florentino could tell himself he had answered the call; he was prepared.

It is significant to read that on his very first assignment as a priest, in the little town of Villaverde, he indicated definitely the course he had chosen for his priestly career: dedication to the sick, the poor, and the penitent; indefatigable effort in teaching Christian Doctrine; devotion to the Sacred Heart of Jesus, and to Our Lady. His love for humanity and his patient skill in the confessional began to win penitents from far and near. When he launched his famous "Bread-for-the-Poor" campaign, those in want knew they had a true father in the young padre.

You must know all about the Little Sisters of the Poor, Saint Sebastian, who devote themselves to taking care of the helpless aged. Was there ever lovelier charity? In the life of Padre Florentino, it seems quite natural to find him soon serving as their chaplain in Valladolid, while assigned to the parish of Saint Ildefonso; and spending many hours in consoling the old men who were their charges. In 1905 he was named chaplain to the Order of the Servants of Jesus; and now feeling certain that his work would keep him in Valladolid, he asked his sister, Francisca, to bring his old parents there so that he might be near them and help them in their last years.

It was not long before word of the great personal sanctity of the obscure young priest reached the ears of the Cardinal Archbishop, Dr. Cos, who startled everyone by appointing him his personal chaplain. New responsibilities were soon added when the Cardinal made him *Mayordomo de Palacio*. It was obvious that these two understood each other, and I love to think, Saint Sebastian, of the humble young priest having found a sympathetic friend in the great Cardinal.

In 1906, Padre Florentino became a teacher of special metaphysics in the Pontifical University, and received his doctorate in theology. Not long after, at the request of the faculty itself, he became a teacher of theology there.

Steadily up the ecclesiastical ladder he rose, this son of a village storekeeper upon whom the Cardinal had come increasingly to depend. But I think that no one who has ever risen up that ladder would say that the ascent is easy; that it is accomplished without casting much of self, and the things of self, by the wayside; without much prayer and human tribulation. By 1915 the Cardinal had appointed him delegate of chaplains, and financial administrator of the diocese. Although it's only a surmise, Saint Sebastian, I imagine that latter post was not too much to his liking, for he had the true saint's distrust of money. He would have liked best to give it all to the poor and have done with it! It was only good for this purpose. It is said that later when he became a bishop, anyone in need could borrow from him unconditionally; that he would accept no receipt, nor set a time for repayment.

The Cardinal's trust was made more evident when in 1918 Father Florentino was appointed Canon of the Cathedral of Valladolid. The Cardinal had come to look upon him as a son; and when in 1919 the distinguished churchman died, his will named Florentino as a beneficiary. It is easy to guess what he did with the bequest. Some of his beloved poor surely benefited. One is certain, understanding the warm and loyal heart of this son of Villasexmir, that he grieved deeply at the passing of his friend.

Valladolid's new archbishop, Dr. Gandasegui, must have shared his predecessor's confidence in Father Florentino, for not long after he was appointed rector of the Cathedral. Now began those long and fruitful years of preaching and expounding the Christian Doctrine. It is said, Saint Sebastian, that he was not a great orator but that he preached with such utter humility and simplicity, making his points with so much practical common sense, that the Cathedral was always crowded to the doors when he preached; that people came from long distances to hear him. There was something about Padre Florentino that won all hearts. One of his most famous sermons was a triduum in honor of Saint Philip Neri—"The Three Loves of Saint Philip: the Blessed Eucharist, Our Lady, and Purity"—which was published and won wide acclaim.

But in all these honors and advancements, he seems never to have relaxed on the first course he had chosen as a young priest. It is said that he sacrificed sleep and food to spend longer hours in the confessional. Souls, always souls; they must be brought back to Christ! And there were those daily visits to the sick. One wonders how in each day he was able to accomplish so much, until one stumbles upon the fact that he had a passion for promptness; that he was one of those enviable souls who know to the minute how to apportion their time. (Alas, Saint Sebastian—but let's not go into all that. We're considering Don Florentino's virtues; not another's shortcomings.)

At this period in Spain, in the early nineteen twenties, the attention of the Church was becoming increasingly centered upon the problems of the workers. An organization of Catholic workers had been formed in Valladolid, to give practical elementary instruction to those who had been forced early to earn their own bread, and to offer them classes in typing, in the arts, and in religion. It was as though the Church, troubled by the unequal economic conditions of the land, had sensed the imminent danger threatening the souls of the underprivileged who would fall an easy prey to the germ of Communism—some of whom indeed were already infected with that black plague. For thirteen years, Father Florentino was indefatigable as counselor to a large group of women workers; not without trouble and dissension which threatened the organization from the start, but which he successfully surmounted after patient vigilance and a diplomacy to be envied by any statesman. The organization grew and expanded, doing its much needed work, and at least in that corner of Valladolid, an immunity to the deadly germ had been built up. Every night, he conducted large classes in Christian Doctrine. "If we don't form truly Christian consciences," he said, "we have wasted our time."

It is delightful to read, Saint Sebastian, that he understood so well the human aspirations of these working girls. He had the positive brilliance to establish a large "dowry box" into which each woman worker put her savings. When the happy day of marriage loomed, each would receive her savings back with interest, and every bride was the proud possessor of a dowry. Only Padre Florentino would have thought of that! The girls looked to the gentle priest with the deep understanding eyes and the ready laugh, in all their problems. It may be that some of them guessed that the secret of his power lay not in his scholar's mind, but simply in prayer. Somehow he arranged his time so that long hours could be spent alone before the Blessed Sacrament. Altar boys who served as he daily celebrated Mass felt this power also; and in one case at least, merely this act of attendance resulted in the re-shaping of one young wayward soul. Padre Florentino had said nothing. He had merely been *himself*, on the altar. It would seem, Saint Sebastian, as though no one could be near him without feeling in a manner sanctified. And always he continued to laugh at himself.

There was that matter of his singing. Like so many charming people who love music and yet who cannot carry a tune, he had a passion for singing. And especially, during the month of May, those lovely hymns to Our Lady. But once when he undertook to lead these hymns before her altar, he noticed a look of alarm on the faces of his flock. It suddenly occurred to Father Florentino that he was stridently off key! He stopped immediately, and when he could leave the church, was the one to laugh the longest at the discordance he had unwittingly raised before the altar of one he loved so deeply.

When those sinister political upheavals forced the Jesuits to leave Spain, the Archbishop asked Father Florentino to serve as rector of one of their churches which otherwise would be abandoned. He was happily fulfilling this task, endearing himself more and more to the people of Valladolid, when one day in October of 1935 he was suddenly called to

Avila, where Monsignor Tedeschini informed him that he had been named Bishop of Barbastro.

Humble and simple as he was, Saint Sebastian, one can imagine his consternation. To be a bishop was the last thing he had ever dreamed of, and he felt totally unworthy. He would just like to remain with his flock and his poor in Valladolid. But when he stammered this desire to the astonished Monsignor, he was told very firmly that he could not fail to comply with the wishes of the Holy Father. As he continued to expostulate, the Monsignor waved off further protests. "Don't give any more excuses," said he. "I merely communicate the will of the Pope. The rest you can tell God in your prayers." And that was that. Poor Father Florentino! He returned to Valladolid a very sad and worried man. He had never been cut out to be a bishop—he, the son of a poor shopkeeper—he told himself.

And although Barbastro then was threatened by the revolution, and although he knew that the plague of Communism had stricken many in the diocese, it was not these causes which gave him the greatest uneasiness. It was simply that he deemed himself unworthy.

Nevertheless, with an inescapable firmness, he was consecrated Bishop of Barbastro, on January 26, 1936. His humility only increased. He could never remember to take the precedence accorded to a bishop. When his own brother, Father Cipriano, visited him to congratulate him on his preferment, Bishop Florentino insisted that he say the grace at table. "You're older than I am," he explained.

But the people of Valladolid were as jubilant as was his brother that so fitting an honor had come to their beloved padre, although they sorrowed at the thought of losing him. The diocese of Barbastro seemed very far away! Sometimes in those days, when alone with his friends, he would sigh, and ask: "And all this, for what?" He did not know then, Saint Sebastian, that it was for something glorious—for Christian martyrdom. And yet he had always revered you and the other great martyrs, with deep devotion. Many had often heard him say: "To give one's life for Christ, is the greatest thing one can do in the world."

It was almost two months after his consecration, months in which matters in far-away Barbastro had grown increasingly worse, that the new bishop was able to leave Valladolid to take over his diocese. And only on that last day, with his saddened friends about him, did he seem to have a premonition of what was to befall. For when one of them protested that he would be entering a dangerous land, he said simply: "What of that? If it comes to being killed, I will only enter Heaven all the sooner!"

Yet Bishop Barroso had no idea then, Saint Sebastian, how very soon that would be. Nor how infected with the fatal plague was his diocese, lying off there in the Pyrenees—the small city of Barbastro, and the widely flung villages comprising something under two hundred parishes. To visit them would be a task, going in and out of the mountains over rough roads, to see to the spiritual welfare of those simple shepherds and farmers.

With his brother and a few others of his household, he arrived in Barbastro on the fourteenth of March, 1936, an evil hour in Spain. Quietly and unostentatiously he took over the episcopal palace; and significantly selected as the theme for his first sermon in the Cathedral: "There shall be one flock, and one Shepherd." But he had come too late. The black plague of Communism had stricken the flock and scattered it. It was running madly, heading for the abyss. Death stalked it. Abuse and sacrilege met Bishop Barroso's Good Shepherd at every turn.

Of course there were thousands of loyal Catholics in Barbastro, and these welcomed their new bishop with open arms. With the same simplicity which had conquered Valladolid, he immediately won their hearts, walking on foot through the streets, and greeting everyone as he had when a young parish priest in the far-off days of Villaverde. How long ago that must have seemed to him now, Saint Sebastian. Spain had changed in the intervening thirty-five years.

The meetings to which the Bishop immediately called all the priests of his diocese revealed a state of affairs ripe for revolution. Not only was there great poverty among the people of hills and city; not only was there a dearth of priests and many empty churches; not only were the priests themselves hungry and threadbare; but the seminary of Barbastro, the fountainhead of religion in all the diocese, was again threatened by the local anticlericals. The Bishop listened sadly as they told him how it had been forcibly entered some time before, and how the seminarians had been forced to flee for their lives. They had only dared return a few months before his arrival. Now their persecutors had plans afoot to demolish it utterly. The Masons and the radicals had gained political control of the city, inflaming the populace, and spreading their incendiary propaganda out into the towns and villages.

Could any bishop have been presented with a more discouraging picture, Saint Sebastian? But the accounts relate that he set to work with accelerated vigor, providing food for the poor, forming an organization for the workers, organizing centers of Christian Doctrine with regular meetings in each parish, assembling all the children for instructions in preparation for their first Holy Communion. Never before had the diocese of Barbastro seen such progress. The very Cathedral seemed to smile; but the smile on the face of Bishop

Florentino was seen less frequently. From signs and portents, he knew that he had come too late. And already he loved these people. Could he but save them! Meantime his sound common sense told him to remove all valuables, paintings and books, from the seminary. He had striven diplomatically to ward off the threatened destruction and had partially succeeded; but he knew it was only for a matter of time.

His priests now became fearful of appearing in the streets in clerical garb. I must say, Saint Sebastian, that from all we know about Spain in those days, one could hardly blame them. But the Bishop saw things differently, sternly rebuking those who asked permission to wear civil attire. It is pleasant to reflect that, in those worrisome days, he enjoyed at least one quiet joke of his own making. When one of the more timid priests who had been called to attend a meeting of radicals asked permission to appear in layman's clothing, the Bishop granted the request, but quickly added:

"It might also be wise to wear a brilliantly colored silk handkerchief in your pocket, and to see that it is heavily perfumed!"

The poor, threadbare cleric looked a bit startled.

Then in May came the long threatened attack upon the seminary. The plague-infected mob completely demolished it. By this time everyone must have been thinking that the Bishop's palace would come next. But if Bishop Florentino thought so, he gave no sign. Bravely, his first Pastoral Letter had appeared in April: a re-emphasis of his first sermon in the Cathedral, "One Flock and One Shepherd." Now immediately following the tragedy of the seminary, appeared his second, and last: a moving plea for re-Christianization of the diocese, with the Catechism as foundation. And ever and always, devotion to the Sacred Heart. But it was still too late.

For in Barbastro, the enemies of Christ had been too long

and too carefully nurturing the germs of the black plague called Communism. At dawn on Sunday, July 19, the revolution took over Barbastro. One thinks of the holy man who was its bishop, hearing the first tumult in the streets—understanding that it had come at last. Feverishly he hurried into his clothes. He must give an example of courage to the others. It was the feast day of Saint Vincent de Paul, he remembered, and he had promised to celebrate Mass at the school dedicated to this saint. He would openly leave the palace and walk to the school. Brushing off the protests of his frightened household, in no time he was in the thick of the seething streets. Miraculously, no one molested him. As he hurried to the school, the thought came to him that it had only been four months since he arrived in Barbastro to take over the spiritual leadership of this tumultuous throng. The sound of firing came to him from a nearby street. Obviously, he hadn't been very successful. And I can imagine that he enjoyed a little rueful smile at his own expense.

In spite of the tumult, a small devoted group waited in the chapel. Never had he said Mass more reverently. When he turned to preach, he uttered words of comfort to the quaking congregation, and urged them gently to pray unceasingly in the peril that had come upon them and their city. Somehow, he got back unharmed to his residence.

A few hours later at noon, word reached him that one of his priests, Father José Martinez, had been arrested and imprisoned. Immediately he sent his vicar-general, the Reverend Félix Sanz, to the Municipal Council, to issue a formal protest in his name. Father Sanz never returned. With several other priests and laymen on that terrible Sunday, he was seized and held prisoner. Finally in the late afternoon, the Municipal Council sent its reply to his message. He was informed that not only was Father Sanz a prisoner, but that he himself was the prisoner of the Council, and forbidden to leave his palace. Events had moved very rapidly in the city of Barbastro, on that hot Sunday in July of 1936.

One can imagine his anxiety for his priests and his flock as, a prisoner in his own house, he spent long hours on his knees, praying constantly for those he loved. Monday and Tuesday passed with ever more alarming tidings. And then on Wednesday, there came two men, knocking on his door. He was told that his palace was needed to serve as a jail; that he must come quickly and just as he was, without any luggage—he, his steward and his chaplain. And I'm certain, Saint Sebastian, that as he left that ill-fated house, he knew he would never return.

Under guard, the silent little party was conducted to an empty schoolhouse, there to be joined by other victims, hazards to the Communist cause because they followed Christ: some twenty-four Benedictine monks, some missionaries, and others whose only crime was that they had tried to do the work of the Good Shepherd in the world.

At first, for a day or so, it was possible to celebrate Mass behind closed doors in the school chapel, to pray for hours before the Blessed Sacrament. The Bishop consoled all, led them in prayer. Then on Friday there arose outside a great tumult in the streets. Cries of "kill them! kill them!" seemed to penetrate the schoolhouse. Panic seized the poor religious. Many of them rushed from the building. Only the Bishop and a few others remained calmly awaiting the event. But it did not come then. The cry had actually been "kill him!" directed at a courageous victim, a magnificent Spanish priest who after terrible torture stood there in the public square and announced firmly to the mob that he was not afraid of any of them.

From then on, it was all so terrible, Saint Sebastian, that my fingers falter, as I try to write; and yet it belongs to the story of Bishop Barroso and I must write it, if only to tell you and him what a rich banner of courage he flung out for the inspiration of Christians everywhere. As awful as had been the events up to now, they were to sink that same afternoon to even lower depths. For there marched into town a section of the Communist-led revolutionary army, and with it those horrible creatures—a species of harpy—those women dressed as men and alas, inflamed with a savagery unequalled in man. At the head of the column, walked one man, Durruti. The Marxist army, having sent their agents in advance, now took over Barbastro. This was a section of the army about which we used to read in our newspapers here, Saint Sebastian, and which, in that either badly informed or unduly influenced press of that time, was dubbed with unconscious irony, "the Loyalist Army."

Arrived in Barbastro, one of their first acts was to commandeer all the mattresses in the school. The poor religious tried to secrete the Bishop's mattress, but he would have none of that. He would sleep on the floor with the rest, if indeed permitted to sleep at all.

There was no sleep that night. The priests knew they could no longer celebrate Mass, so the Hosts were broken into many small pieces, that each might partake of Holy Communion as long as possible. Outside in the streets, the Communist mob howled and swirled like demons, in and out of the churches, smashing images and shrines, pillaging, spreading sacrilege and desecration. The black plague was raging with the fury of hell. From a window, the Bishop looked sadly down upon his city of Barbastro, and prayed.

I do not know on which one of the horrible days that followed, that Durruti advanced his barbaric proposal. Determined to have the lives of all the clergy, and in particular the Bishop's, and casting about for a good reason to give the populace, he arose one day and from a balcony of the Municipal Council delivered a speech. In it he loudly protested that he had just learned that a short time before the local Communist committee had put to death two Communists accused of wholesale robbery. Ignoring the fact that, apart from the severity of the punishment, robbery was a crime, he excoriated all of Barbastro for permitting such an outrage against two loyal Communists. Working up to a climax of oratory, he cried:

"For that act, and to equalize matters, I demand the head of your Bishop!"

He went on to explain that he was letting them off easy; that the populace was really getting a bargain. In other words, one Bishop was worth two of Durruti's thieving fellow-travelers. I suppose the Bishop should have felt flattered, as he listened to the whole thing from his window.

Of course Durruti had flung appalling accusations at the Church, and as a result the Bishop was ordered to appear before a so-called tribunal. It was an odd thing, Saint Sebastian, that the tribunal called upon him in the schoolhouse, rather than requiring him to come to them—a definite mark of respect. Regardless of what else had happened since Bishop Florentino had arrived in town, it would seem that in those scant four months, even the most lawless had come to respect that saintly character. The hearing followed the usual tragicomedy pattern of a Red trial. The Bishop was accused of holding meetings with two deputies of the Cortes. He serenely agreed this was true; but that the meetings had not been of a political nature. They had merely discussed the seminary. Considering what had happened to the seminary, this was all Durruti needed.

It was the night of August 8th when he was again called before the tribunal, but this time he was required to go to the offices of the Municipal Council. How weary he must have been after the three long weeks as a prisoner, sleeping on the floor, denied access to his personal belongings, suffering every discomfort while tenderly consoling his unhappy companions. This night he hoped that the tribunal would not keep him long. He could not believe they really intended to harm him. He had only tried to do good in the city of Barbastro. And every day had he not prayed for the souls of those who kept him in custody? Had he not counseled his companions to speak no word of complaint against them?

It is said that there was a room in the Council building, known as the *rastrillo*—a place of detention for prisoners. Here he spent the night, and here his torture was consummated. It is not related how many Communists—members of that "Loyalist Army"—came in and out throughout the night, came to revile and insult him. Nor how many entered there to beat him. But it is related that all these things were perpetrated on the gentle shepherd who now lacked but a year of being sixty. Insults and kicks and beatings were showered on that elderly man, and more. He was cut and tortured, Saint Sebastian, in ways that must remain nameless. For that was the level on which they moved. This was the Communist philosophy carried to its logical end—the diabolical.

When two o'clock came, his wounds were so grievous that he could not walk to his martyrdom; so a hasty therapy was rendered, just sufficient to enable him to walk. Then, with several other victims, he was led out to the cemetery of Barbastro, the cemetery of his episcopal city. And as he stumbled along over the dim road, ignoring the terrible pain, the gibes and insults of his guards, witnesses related that he kept repeating:

"What a beautiful night for me! I am going to the house of my Lord."

And when they shoved and kicked him along, he said:

"I forgive you! I forgive you all! I forgive everyone. When I am in Heaven, I shall pray for you."

Are not those the signs of the true martyr, Saint Sebastian? He was happy because he was going to "witness" for his Lord. He forgave those who tortured him, those who were leading him to death.

The scene at the cemetery is one that has dwelt in horror with me for a long time, Saint Sebastian. Again, my fingers falter, but the vivid picture haunting me must be set down. I can almost smell the damp earth of that eerie place in the pre-dawn air, as I watch the Communists line their victims up near the cemetery chapel. They place one behind another, close together, in a file. That is because the "Loyalist" captain has been boasting all along the way that he need not waste many bullets on them. He is a crack shot, he is! He will show them. He will kill them *all*, with one bullet.

And so the single shot rang out. And each man in the file fell from the one bullet. But the Communist captain was not such a good shot, after all. For one in the line wasn't dead. He lay there groaning and bleeding profusely. Oh, it was only that reactionary old Bishop! Well, let him bleed to death. And so for two long hours he lay there in agony, as the life-blood flowed from him, conscious—and over and over again blessing his enemies. What a "testimony," Saint Sebastian!

"I forgive, I forgive," he murmured. And then weakly: "My Father, open soon to me the door of Heaven!" Perhaps it was those words which caused a "good-natured" Communist guard to waste another bullet, and end his sufferings. He had put on a good "show" for them....

They had enjoyed the show, just as the pagans of Rome, six centuries earlier, had enjoyed the show of watching you bleed to death in the Campus Martius from the wounds of a hundred arrows. Only, you had tricked them. Leaving you for dead, the Mauretanian archers had trotted off to the Emperor Diocletian, whose great favorite you had been until he discovered you were a Christian, to tell him they had done a thorough job on you. Dear Saint Sebastian, the legend of what followed is so recurrent that it must be founded on fact! Somehow you were miraculously healed—some say through the prayers of the widowed Saint Irene—and lived to confront the Emperor a few days later on the steps of his palace. It must have given him a nervous moment.

"Is this not Sebastian, whom we put to death with arrows?" he inquired, his knees shaking.

"The Lord has recalled me to life, so that once more I may come to you and reproach you for the ill you do to the servants of Christ!"

But it was no use. The imperial pride rekindled, Diocletian called his soldiers and stood over them while they beat you to death. And so you entered into the glory of one of the greatest Christian martyrs of all time.

Dear Bishop Barroso must have thought much upon your story, as he prayed there in the prison schoolhouse of Barbastro, for by then he knew that he was being called to Christian martyrdom in the year 1936, as you had been called in the year 286. He would have remembered the young Sebastian whose story is preserved in the Roman Martyrology; and have reflected with admiration that while he was being called to "testify" after a fruitful life at the age of fifty-nine, you were still a youth when the sharp arrows rained upon you. He would have remembered how you had come to Rome from Milan at the request of the Emperor himself who, struck by your valor and handsome appearance, had made you an officer of his own imperial bodyguard.

But particularly would he have recalled how, as a Christian convert, you had gone in and out of the prisons, consoling those Christians who awaited torture and death, strengthening their faith and fortitude by expounding again to them the precepts of the Christian doctrine. That emphasis upon the doctrine! Ah, that was what he himself had considered so important.

Was his present plight not due to the fact that he had established centers of Christian Doctrine throughout the diocese of Barbastro; had conferred with deputies of the Cortes in an effort to preserve the seminary which produced the teachers of Christian Doctrine? He would have understood why you were willing to die for it.

And having heard from his window the fury of the Communist Durruti, demanding his head, he would have comprehended the fury which possessed Diocletian when he learned that his favorite guardsman was disseminating that doctrine. For the doctrine is such that neither the paganism of ancient Rome nor the Communism of today can long survive where it is preached.

And finally, dear Saint Sebastian, he would have appealed to you as do I, to preserve the world from the black plague called Communism which has enslaved so much of God's earth, and has brought about this Second Age of Martyrdom. He would have asked your prayers for our modern martyrs—for Stepinac in a Communist prison in Yugoslavia; for Mindszenty in a Communist prison in Hungary; whose living martyrdoms have been a light to the world, as have been the actual martyrdoms of Father Pro of Mexico, and Bishop Barroso of Spain. These are only four of a multitude who, exposed to the travesty of Soviet "justice," have suffered and died at the hands of those afflicted by that plague and possessed with a determination to destroy the Kingdom of Christ. For love of Christ have these millions accepted torture and death in giving their heroic "testimony."

And so in closing, dear Saint Sebastian, I would ask you who went about the pagan prisons of Rome exhorting the faithful to fidelity, to be at the side of the faithful now in all lands where they and freedom are being persecuted. With you, with all the early martyrs who carved out the pattern of heroism, to pray for them—and with the modern martyrs to inspire them—they cannot fail.

POSTSCRIPT to MARTYRS

It was through the generous helpfulness of many friends that I came to learn about you, the heroes of the First and Second Ages of Martyrdom. Indeed, it was from these that I drew courage to write you. There is no better way to show my gratitude than to petition you in their behalf, asking your prayers for these, my friends.

The list which follows is incomplete because, you see, God has been very good to me in the matter of friends. It is not possible to enumerate all who helped me in this epistolary endeavor; but a few are listed below whose kindness, patience, and help were inexhaustible:

The Religious of Marymount College, New York;

Mother Frawley and Mother Lonergan, and the Religious of the Cenacle of St. Regis, New York City;

Reverend Godfrey Wolf, O.F.M.Conv., of Seaside Park, N.J.;

Reverend Francis X. Talbot, S.J., of Georgetown University, brilliant authority on Martyrs;

Reverend Ralph Gorman, C.P., distinguished Editor of the *Sign;*

Reverend Edward A. Conway, S.J., Associate Editor of *America;*

Reverend John Joseph Considine, M.M., of Maryknoll, N.Y.;

Reverend Florence D. Cohalan, of Cathedral College, New York;

Reverend Marian Wöjcik, O.F.M.Conv., of New York City;

Reverend José Antonio Sobrino, S.J., of Georgetown University;

Miss Julie Kernan, of the David McKay Company, New York City, but for whose expert, patient, and tireless collaboration these letters would never have been written;

Prince Jan Drucki Lubecki of New York City;

Mr. Anthony Atar, of New York City;

Mr. Akos Zombory, co-author of *The Communist Wars on Religion*, just published by the Devin-Adair Company, New York City;

Miss Leona Marie Segebrecht, of New York, to whom I owe the biographical material on Father Delp of Germany, and who graciously permitted quotations from her translation of Father Delp's book, *In the Face of Death*, in which she is currently engaged;

Señor Enrique Videgain Cordova, consul-general of Panama, at Barcelona, Spain;

Señor Francisco Moncayo, of the Spanish Consulate-General, New York;

Miss Consuelo Ballesteros, skilful translator of the biography of Bishop Barroso of Spain;

Paul J. Haas, colleague in research;

Miss Eleanor Sherman Fitch, Miss Mary Kolars, Miss Clare Faulhaber, of New York; Miss Margaret Fitzgerald, of Boston, collaborators in research;

Frank A. Hall, Director, NCWC News Service, Washington, D.C., and many others of the faithful whose devotion to you and kindness to me was proved a thousand times in the course of this correspondence.

H.W.H.

BIBLIOGRAPHY

Allard, Paul. *Ten Lectures on the Martyrs.* New York: Benziger Bros., 1907.

Arranz, C.M.F., Revdo P. Antonio M. *Obispo y Mártir.* Barbastro, Spain, 1947. From the English trans. by Consuelo Ballesteros.

Atar, Anthony B. "Forgotten Builders of New Germany," in the *Sign,* April, 1950, pp. 34-7.

Buehle, Marie Cecilia. *Saint Maria Goretti.* Milwaukee: The Bruce Publishing Co., 1950.

Butler, Rev. Alban. *The Lives of the Saints.* Edited by Herbert Thurston, S.J., and Donald Attwater. New York: P. J. Kenedy & Sons, 1934.

Cardinal Mindszenty Speaks (*Authorized White Book*). New York: Longmans, Green & Co., 1949.

Considine, M.M., John Joseph. *When the Sorghum was High.* New York: Longmans, Green & Co., 1940.

Delp, S.J., Alfred. *In the Face of Death.* Now in process of translation by Leona Marie Segebrecht.

Fabian, Bela. *Cardinal Mindszenty.* New York: Charles Scribner's Sons, 1949.

Forrest, M.S.C., Rev. M.D. *The Life of Father Pro.* St. Paul: Radio Replies Press, 1945.

Halecki, Oscar. *Eugenio Pacelli: Pope of Peace.* New York: Creative Age Press, 1951.

Lake, Kirsopp (ed.). *The Apostolic Fathers.* New York: G. P. Putnam's Sons, 1919.

Lebreton, Jules. *The History of the Primitive Church.* New York: The Macmillan Co., 1924.

Maguire, C. E. *Maria Goretti.* New York: Catholic Book Publishing Co., 1950.

Markham, R. H. *Tito's Imperial Communism.* Chapel Hill, N. C.: University of North Carolina Press, 1947.

McSorley, C.S.P., Joseph. *Outline History of the Church by Centuries.* St. Louis: B. Herder Book Co., 1948.

Norman, Mrs. George. *God's Jester.* New York: Benziger Bros., 1930.

O'Brien of Thomond, Count. *Archbishop Stepinac, the Man and his Case.* Westminster, Md.: The Newman Bookshop, 1947.

The Red Domination in Spain. Drawn up by the Ministry of Justice. Madrid: Afrodisio Aguado, S.A., 1946.

Repplier, Agnes. *In Pursuit of Laughter.* Boston: Houghton Mifflin Co., 1936.

Rimmer, S.J., John. *Father Miguel Pro, S.J.* London: Catholic Truth Society, 1921.

Shipkov, Michael. *Breakdown.* New York: National Committee for Free Europe, 1950.

Swift, Stephen K. *The Cardinal's Story.* New York: The Macmillan Co., 1949.

Voragine, Jacobus de. *The Golden Legend.* Translated by Granger Ryan and Helmut Ripperger. New York: Longmans, Green & Co., 1941.

Winowska, Maria. *Le Fou de Notre Dame.* Paris: La Bonne Presse, 1950.